THE
BLACK
FRIEND

First published 2021 by Walker Books Ltd
87 Vauxhall Walk, London SE11 5HJ

2 4 6 8 10 9 7 5 3 1

This book has been typeset in Chaparral Pro and Trade Gothic

Printed and bound by CPI Group (UK) Ltd, Croydon CR0 4YY

British Library Cataloguing in Publication Data:
a catalogue record for this book is available
from the British Library

ISBN 978-1-5295-0061-5

www.walker.co.uk

MIX
Paper from
responsible sources
FSC® C020471

THE
BLACK
FRIEND

ON BEING
A BETTER
WHITE
PERSON

FREDERICK JOSEPH

WALKER
BOOKS

To my mother and grandmother,

who made sure this Black boy knew he was amazing——

even when the world tried to teach him otherwise

Brandon, this book is for you

and millions of other Black and brown children

who should be loved for all of your beauty and glory.

CONTENTS

PREFACE

To My Reader:

I finished writing *The Black Friend* in 2019, but so much has happened in 2020, I feel like I have to address it. Though we are only six months in as I write this, this year has already had a historic impact on the entire world.

When I wrote this book, I had one goal in mind: try to help make things better. In the case of racism and white supremacy, the word *better* is difficult to define. This is because, as discussed throughout this book, racism and white supremacy influence literally everything. Therefore, *better* is always a matter of perspective based on what a person is dealing with.

Racism and white supremacy are the root causes of world-altering moments, such as the murder of Michael Brown in 2014, as well as subtle moments, such as a white woman clutching her purse closely when I enter an elevator.

In the first case, *better* would be defined as the police no longer murdering Black people. In the other, *better* would be defined as white women no longer leaning into racist stereotypes about Black men.

Though they are both racist moments, it's obviously difficult to compare the two. But both cases do share one common denominator: the humanity of Black people being stripped away.

This may all be difficult to understand for some—but that is exactly why I wrote this book. Its success will be defined not by how many copies are sold, but rather by how much *better* people are for having read it.

My hope is that this book will be a tool to help others see and understand the obvious and not-so-obvious ways in which racism and white supremacy not only have infected our society but are actually the foundation of it. That it might spark the flame in someone who one day helps burn down the historic oppression we have faced.

But a lot has changed (and so much has stayed the same) since I wrote this book, and while I still hold those same hopes, I am also tired. So incredibly tired.

As I sit here contemplating the words I might use to explain to you how detrimental 2020 has been to the souls of Black people, I find myself unable to write them. Not because there aren't countless thoughts floating through my mind that could be shared. But rather because I don't want to give them to you.

This isn't an attempt to be disrespectful, as much as an attempt to explain just how tired I am. In this book I've already given my readers so much—my pain, my trauma, and my life—in hopes that maybe future Black generations won't have to do the same.

I don't want to use the very little energy I have left talking to non-Black people about this moment in time.

Instead, I would rather help Black children understand it. Children like my eight-year-old brother.

So I will write to him, and you may take from it what you will.

. . . .

My Brother, Brandon:

By the time you read this, you'll likely be about twelve years old, though you're a very gifted child, so maybe you'll be a bit younger. Either way, I hope I'm still alive to see it and to talk to you about it, about why I felt compelled to write it. Though, with the way things are going, I'm not sure I will be.

I saw you recently in the midst of everyone trying to survive the pandemic and protesting for social justice, and as usual you didn't have a care in the world. As it should be for an eight-year-old.

I wish that I could make it so that your life was always that way, but it won't be long before the stress of being Black in this world finds you.

I am heartbroken by this unchangeable fact.

As I write this, you are still too young to understand that to be Black in America is to be left with two options: either you pretend oppression isn't happening or you fight back.

I say pretend *because there is no way that any Black person who is born in this house, which is on fire, and always has been, doesn't come to realize that smoke is filling their lungs.*

That smoke is the reason, when you were six years old, our mother had to report one of your teachers for looking at the labels of your clothes to check whether they were real. Because she couldn't fathom that a Black child could be the best dressed student in a predominantly white class in the suburbs.

That smoke is why at such a young age you had already been taught to assess when a white person was doing something so blatantly racist.

That smoke is why I have so many stories to tell about my own traumatic moments. Far more than any person should ever have.

But the smoke is just a symptom. What's destroying the house—what's destroying us*—is racism and white supremacy.*

You deserve better, and I deserved better—and now, I demand better. Which is why I've chosen to use every resource at my disposal to fight back. As long as I have a platform, I will use it to make our voices heard. I will write, so long as it's the truth.

And as our people put their lives at risk marching in the street for justice, I must be with them.

But by choosing to fight back, I have only increased the likelihood of being taken from you, as so many of my idols before me were taken from their loved ones. Such is the reality in this land where Black people are murdered for simply existing.

While I haven't said it directly to her, I feel a deep sorrow for the position I've put our mother in, or rather the position this country has put her in. She must live with the gravity of loving me, and of loving our people. Which means she understands that she may be forced to sacrifice something.

I'm sure who I've become is no surprise to her; she raised me with the values that got me here, that made me the loud, staunch, and aggressive anti-racist I am today. This is why she has never asked me to stop my work, as fearful as I know she is. Why she understood me protesting when police murdered Akai Gurley, even though I was arrested for doing so. Why she didn't object when I told her I was going to write a book to help white people unlearn white supremacy. Why she simply walks away in silence when she hears about the weekly emails I receive calling me a nigger.

But having been through all of that, 2020 is still different for us both. The weight is heavier, the sacrifices are greater, and the fires are as large as ever.

Before, when Mommy and I would talk on the phone, we would end our conversations with a goodbye and an occasional "I love you." Now we have an unsaid agreement not to hang up without saying that we love each other. We both know we are living in a time when we might not get another chance to say those words.

This is particularly true in my case, as we are living through COVID-19, a global pandemic that has taken the lives of hundreds of thousands of people—especially people like me, who are immunocompromised. The same pandemic that has ravaged the Black community more than any other, because of the historic inequities in America.

It's a humbling feeling to go to sleep every night hoping to not get sick. Which is why I've been extremely diligent and careful during this time for my safety, because I understand how serious it is, and I want to be here.

"Are you wearing a mask? Are you using antibacterial soap? Are you staying away from other people?" Mommy has called me every day for the last four months asking me the same questions, trying to make sure I don't get sick. Trying to make sure her eldest son doesn't become another victim of a virus that has already disproportionately decimated the Black community and furthered the health, wealth, and education gaps in this country.

The feeling that your life may potentially be lost at any moment to a virus is a frightening one, though it's not much different from the feeling of any Black person who fears they may never see their loved ones again whenever they step outside. Not because accidents happen to Black people but rather because hatred happens to Black people.

Hatred happened to Ahmaud Arbery, Breonna Taylor, Tony

McDade, George Floyd, and David McAtee. They are the most recent high-profile cases of Black people who have been murdered by white supremacists, and their deaths are the reason why millions of people around the world are risking their lives to demand justice.

Protests aren't new; neither are marches, or riots. But this moment we are in is unprecedented. Never before have we seen people so overtly weighed down by this many oppressive systems at one time. While we have to worry about losing our jobs and feeding our children during a pandemic, we also have to worry about those same children being shot by the police while playing outside.

More people than ever have had enough and are fighting back. I'm proud to be one of them.

This is inherently the burden of those who are oppressed. As I write this, there is no vaccine for COVID-19; people are still at risk, getting sick, and losing their lives. But Black bodies being left hanging from trees or dead in the street is an older and more insidious problem, and the opportunity to defeat it has once again presented itself.

As a Black man, I don't get to worry about being immuno-compromised during COVID-19, not while a police officer kneels on George Floyd's neck until he dies.

As a Black woman, our mother doesn't get to tell her son not to go protest for justice, not while Breonna Taylor is murdered by police officers as she sleeps in her bed.

We don't get to unpack our fear of white supremacists

lashing out while at these protests, not while Ahmaud Arbery is gunned down by white supremacists for simply jogging.

White supremacy. Racism. Police brutality. A global pandemic. Staggering job losses. A white supremacist in the Oval Office. Only halfway into the year, and 2020 has already been the combination of everything that is wrong with this country happening all at once.

But as they say, it is darkest before dawn.

In every state and around the world, people have begun to rise against the tyranny of white supremacy.

Ultimately, that darkness will take some of us, as it always has. None of us know what's going to happen. But I wanted you to know that when things got so dark and so bleak and we were pushed against the wall—we pushed back.

No more police brutality. No more white supremacy. No more Black bodies.

We were prepared to pay the costs, prepared to make the sacrifices that were necessary. I don't know whether I will be sacrificed, and believe me, I don't romanticize the idea. I want to live. We all do. Don't let them tell you any different.

But if sacrifice means victory, a chance for liberation, a future in which you never have to write a letter like this, then it would have been well worth it.

Love,

Your Big Brother

June 2020

INTRODUCTION

One of the most important lessons I learned when I was younger was that being a Black person in this world usually means that at some point, you're going to have to do things you don't enjoy. Even more important was learning that many of those things are going to involve white people.

For me, that has meant spending a lot of my time as an adult discussing white supremacy, **white privilege**, and the negative aspects of whiteness in general.

> ▶▶ If you don't know what a bolded word or term means, don't worry: I've defined it at the back of the book. Yes, friends: it's your very own Encyclopedia of Racism.

Anyone who truly knows me would tell you I'd much rather spend my time tweeting about the Lakers, watching rom-coms, or sleeping. But, as I learned a long time ago, there aren't enough people addressing societal issues, so here I am.

Because of how publicly critical I am of the impact white people have, and have had, on people of color and on the general world around them, some people have gone so far as to say I hate white people.

Honestly, this deeply offends me, as I've been to over ten John Mayer concerts and at least two hockey games; there's no way a person who hates white people willingly attends the two whitest events on earth multiple times.

That said, my one actual problem with white people is that many just don't have any sense of accountability when it comes to people of color. Accountability not only for the things white people do that often make interacting with them the most frustrating and tumultuous part of our days. But also, accountability for the historic and current inequities and disparities plaguing Black people and people of color as a whole.

Which is why I've written this book. Not because of the fame, fortune, and chance to meet Oprah—though those would be pretty dope. But, as a Black person, I speak on behalf of people of color (except those of us on Fox News) when I say: WE HAVE A WHITE PEOPLE PROBLEM.

My aim is to help you go from being a person who is learning and unlearning things about these problems created and perpetuated by white people to someone who actively works to solve them. This is called being an anti-racist.

I define anti-racists as people who understand that white supremacy isn't something to empathize with Black

and brown people over. It's a destructive system and exis-
tence that white people created, and anti-racists are
actively trying to end it.

While many believe there is no way to change the problem, because they believe there is no way to change white
people, I disagree. Because after sitting with and talking to
many white people throughout my life, I've come to realize
that there are white people who do care and who I believe
want to make change. But these same white people often
don't understand the negative impact they are having or
how to be better, because many of them have never had the
conversations necessary to know this stuff, either in the
classroom or outside of it.

Let's face it: Black people and people of color are taught in
school, in the media, and in everyday interactions to be empathetic and understanding of white people and their history. But
most white people never have to do the same for us.

> 🚩 You'll notice I don't capitalize the *w* in white when
> referring to white people, though I capitalize the *B* when
> referring to Black people. This is a personal preference,
> because white people are simply defined by the color of their
> skin, while Black people are a cultural and ethnic group.

For example, I've never met a white person who doesn't
know who Christopher Columbus was (even though he didn't
discover anything). But most white people can't have an

informed conversation about the indigenous people who were already in America and the lingering impact on indigenous people today of so many of their ancestors having been slaughtered by people like Christopher Columbus. Nor do most white people know anything about the white supremacist massacre of Black people in Tulsa, Oklahoma—though most white people can tell you that Kevin Durant and Russell Westbrook played together on the Oklahoma City Thunder.

To put it plainly, we have to learn a lot of white crap, including white history, much of which is not even true. Meanwhile, white people never have to learn about us, because doing so would force white people to be held accountable for the many ways they've mistreated—and continue to mistreat—people of color.

This book is an opportunity to change that. To provide some of the context and history that is so often lacking for white people.

Heck, we even added the Encyclopedia of Racism because my white editor pointed out that many of you reading this might not understand some of the terms that I'll be using, some of the events I refer to, or why certain things are racist.

▶▶ I hope you already looked up **white privilege**, from page 17. Here's another opportunity to use the encyclopedia: if you aren't familiar with the 1921 **Tulsa Race Massacre**, go to the back of the book and learn about it.

But to the point about people who think white people can't change: I understand, and have met those white people, too. These are the types of white people who will say things like "Black people need to get over slavery" or "We had a Black president; there is no more racism." These are people who want white supremacy to continue because it benefits them. They are the same people who will say this book sucks, never having read it.

But this book isn't for those white people. It's for the ones who want to do better, who want to *be* better. But where do white people start? How does someone learn empathy? Is it by watching a specific movie? Listening to an album?

I think it starts with understanding.

. . . .

I'll never forget the first day of my sophomore year of high school. I had just transferred from a school that was primarily Black to a new school that was far more white. I was prepared for the shock of just how many white people there were going to be in my everyday now. What I was not prepared for was how shocked they were going to be by me. There were other people of color in the school, yes, but I was one of the only Black transfer students. Being one of very few transfer students was probably enough to make me stand out, but being a transfer student who wasn't *white* pretty much guaranteed that I'd be noticed.

Because I transferred at the beginning of my sophomore year, the students in my school had already grown accustomed to one another, and everyone seemed to have their role. I quickly learned what people assumed my role would be.

During my first lunch period, I sat by myself. This lasted for about fifteen minutes, until a group of slightly older white kids walked over. They sat at my table and stared at me, and one eventually asked what school I transferred in from.

I looked at them for a second and told them.

"Oh, that's the ghetto school," one replied. "Lucky you made it here."

I didn't even know how to process that.

I sat in the silence, still surprised that a wild pack of white boys were speaking to me in the first place. Before I could respond, another asked me a question that gives context to my entire experience while at the school and, for a long time, my views on white people and my very self.

"What hood do you live in?"

This wasn't meant to be a friendly way of finding out whether we were from the same area; this was an assumption, or rather an assertion. "Hood" was slang for a low-income area, and in the part of the country where we lived (Yonkers, New York), those areas were typically filled with Black and Latinx people.

> **ⅠⅠ** You'll see me use *Latinx* in the book, as it's a gender-neutral term for people who are Latin American.

Can't ask people to respect my people if I don't respect theirs, right?

But not all Black and Latinx people lived in the "hood," and this white boy had never spoken to me or even met me, so he couldn't have had any idea about where I was from or how much money my family had. He simply assumed I was poor and lived in a "hood" because I was Black.

II This is a common racist **stereotype** about nonwhite people. But in reality, **most people living in poverty in America are white**.

But I was fifteen years old and wanted to fit in, and he wasn't wrong—I was from a "hood." So I told them where I was from, and they immediately thought I was cool and edgy. That was the day I became the token Black guy.

II A token Black guy or girl is a Black person that white people can claim they know in order to avoid being called racist and who doesn't ever make them feel uncomfortable about the racist things they do. Kind of like Kanye West and the Kardashian family.

To add context, this was in 2004, before there was social media, a Black president and First Lady, and trendy **wokeness**. It was basically the Wild West. It wasn't MAGA bad, at least not on the surface, but it was a different type of bad: an I-don't-realize-what-I'm-saying-or-doing-is-hella-problematic-and-racist bad.

In my first few weeks at that high school, I quickly learned that there were only a few ways white people viewed people of color, and we were broken into specific groups:

If you were Black, that meant you were unquestionably good at sports, even if no one had seen you play yet. You grew up in an impoverished neighborhood, you came from a single-parent home, you knew every rap song ever made, you were prone to violence or stealing, and you had no interest in academics.

For Latinxs, it was assumed that your first language was Spanish, you had a large number of siblings, you were proficient in Latin dancing, and you were probably in some type of gang.

Asian kids had stereotypes placed on them that might seem positive—they're often referred to as the "model minority"—but stereotypes are inherently problematic. The East Asian students in my school, and in schools across the country, were seen as being highly intelligent, mild mannered, and more than likely to know martial arts.

While I often make the point that no one in the world has it worse than Black people in regard to stereotypes and racism, in the early 2000s, people from the Middle East had it *bad*. At that point, we were only a few years removed from September 11, and people were not only racist, they were racist on steroids. They would vandalize the homes and businesses of Muslims and people perceived as Muslim, attack their places of worship, and gang up on them and beat them up. All in the name of "American values." Most of the physical abuse wasn't taking place in my school, but the mental and verbal abuse certainly was.

Because much of what was going on in the world was also taking place in my school, it was a very difficult place to be a student of color. Not only did we have to worry about fitting in, but we also had to worry about surviving in a place that was obviously not meant for us. But, as we'll discuss throughout the book, my school wasn't much different from America generally.

Many of us had messed-up experiences during that time. But I think the worst part was that we started to become *conditioned* to many of the stereotypes and problematic views about our groups.

Including myself.

That's not to say I thought I was a murderous thief or naturally great at basketball (especially because I was never that great at ball). But I started going along with some things that set the tone for how I viewed and felt about myself for years and, eventually, how I viewed and felt about white people.

Again, like most students, I wanted to fit in and be welcomed. So to do that, I aligned myself with whatever made that process easier, even if it meant growing accustomed to laughing when a white person called me an Oreo (Black on the outside, white on the inside) for enjoying Maroon 5 or letting it go when someone asked me random questions about "the hood" without knowing where I was from.

I was like a cooler version of Carlton from *The Fresh Prince of Bel-Air* or that one Black cast member on each season of *The Real World*. You know, the one who hangs around white people and makes them feel comfortable, even when they do something problematic or racist. The person to whom people say things like "You just happen to be Black." And for all intents and purposes, it worked.

> ⏮ I'm not going to even bother explaining *The Fresh Prince*; if you've never heard of that show, the world has failed you. But there's a chance you don't know what *The Real World* is, which gives me hope for humanity. Basically, it was a reality show on MTV about a group of strangers who were given a house in a random city and asked to live together, and we watched them all hate one another and throw shade. (Dang, I feel old.)

By the time I got to my senior year, not only had I survived by being the token Black kid; I had thrived. I was voted both most popular and prom king by my classmates, and I was the vice president of the student government.

I figured I would carry on this way even after high school. I knew the world was primarily white, so I should just get used to navigating white people's stereotypes and problematic behaviors by pacifying them. I was going to be the token Black guy forever.

Thankfully, I've spent my years since high school learning and meeting people who were far more culturally aware and thoughtful than I was, which helped me realize that the role I wanted to play around white people wasn't the token Black guy but rather "the Black friend."

Let me explain.

I like to think of the high school version of myself as the original Black Power Ranger: well meaning but extremely problematic. While he did have powers and helped save the world, he also was constantly dancing to hip-hop music, rapping, and speaking in slang. It was a very stereotypical representation of Blackness. (They also really had an Asian woman play the Yellow Ranger: yikes.)

The college version of myself was attempting to be a young Stokely Carmichael. My militant pro-Blackness was awakened by writers like James Baldwin and Toni Morrison. I spent most of that time protesting, refusing to speak to most white people in public, and trying to support only Black-owned businesses—it was a great time to be alive.

⏸ I would normally say you should google Stokely Carmichael (later known as Kwame Ture), but I did my own search, and as it often happens with pro-Black figures, the first results about him were falsely negative.

Stokely is famously known for coining the term "Black Power" and was a civil rights leader and grassroots organizer.

The thing about being militant Black and refusing to speak to white people is that it makes it difficult to earn a living. Which is why by the time I was in my early to midtwenties, I became more like Denzel Washington.

⏸ While Denzel is known widely for the movies he's been in and his award-winning acting, behind the scenes he's made a great deal of change for Black people. He's done things such as help students pay for college and has even let young Black people live with him and his family if they need a place to stay. He's also donated millions of dollars to historically Black colleges. And this has all been very under the radar.

But now I think I'm in a moment where I'm a good mix of all of my phases (except that Black Ranger moment, yuck). My focus is on using everything at my disposal, from storytelling to access to finances, to help create a better and freer future for all people of color, especially young people. In large part, this means finding ways to educate and inform the white people who want to listen and grow. I call this my Ava DuVernay phase.

⏸ Ava is the director of films such as the award-winning *Selma*, about the Civil Rights Act of 1964; the documentary *13th*, about the history of race and justice in America; and series such as *When They See Us*, about the Exonerated Five (formerly known as the Central Park Five). You should probably just see everything she's made, to be on the safe side.

Throughout the book, you'll read about moments from each of my personal phases. I'll be speaking to you directly at times to explain certain things and to give my current opinion on stories and conversations you'll be reading about.

I'm also going to be pretty damn hard on my past self.

I call this voice the Black Friend.

. . . .

I often think back to that white kid asking me about my "hood."

Realistically, we were both problematic. He was wrong for making that assumption about me, and likely about many other Black people, and I was wrong for playing into it.

By not telling him that he was wrong to make such an assumption and by instead going along with it, I made him feel like it was fine to do this to me and, worse, to do it to other Black people. I could have said that not all Black people live in a hood, or that not all Black people live in poverty, and

THE BLACK FRIEND

that his question was racist. Hell, I could have also simply said nothing, which would have been better than basically agreeing with the racist stereotype.

I couldn't see any of that at the time, but I see it now, and I've made it the mission of this book to help others to see it, too, by choosing to create the Black Friend. In this context, the Black Friend is the person who is willing to speak the truth to the white people in their lives, to call them out when they do or say something hurtful, ignorant, or offensive. After reading this book, my hope is that white people won't need to tokenize or ask Black people and people of color to do all of the work.

It's not an easy thing, being the Black Friend. And it's certainly not a role every Black person should be expected to take on. But those of us who choose to play that role do so because we know that by helping our white friends become better people, we help make the world a little bit better for the rest of us.

As your Black Friend, in this book I'm going to share— as examples and as a guideline of things *not to do*—some of my personal stories as well as stories from other people of color about problematic moments created by white people.

> ⏸ Much of the dialogue in the scenes from my younger years is invented, as I didn't have a tape recorder running. But I've done my best to be true to the people involved—

30

my past self included—and to the sentiments felt at the time. All names have been changed to protect the not-so-innocent.

This book is meant to provide teaching moments, cultural history, and context for white people. But just as important, this book is also supposed to provide affirmations for people of color—that you are seen and loved. Know that others are dealing with the same stuff. *You are not alone.* This book is also for those of you who may not realize yet what you're dealing with—I was one of those.

I've been using my energy for most of my life to try to make the world a better place, and I'm still fighting the good fight, but frankly, I'm getting my ass kicked. Hell, everyone working to make the world better for people of color is getting their ass kicked, too.

The world needs you to step up, or get out of the way. (Imagine me saying this in my most superhero-monologue-like voice.) *Particularly* if you are a white person. The world needs to be better, and because of the power that white people hold in our society, much of that change needs to start with white people. The oppression that white people have inflicted on people of color since, well, damn, the very inception of this country can only be undone by the oppressors (white people).

If you're reading this, that means you're probably a white person who wants to do better, or a person of color who wants to reaffirm things to feel less alone—or someone who bought this book to burn it. (Yep, I see you—and thanks for the royalties.) But, as you've seen from the title of the book, this is aimed primarily at the first audience I mentioned, the white people who want to be better.

All wise people know that no one knows everything. If you feel you don't need to read this book because you're already a decent white person, there's a good chance you're not as decent as you think.

1

WE WANT YOU TO SEE RACE

Featuring Angie Thomas

There's something special about firsts—you know, your first kiss, a baby's first steps, the first day of school, your first time deleting a message from your teacher so your parents don't know you got in trouble at school.

High school was a time of many firsts for me, but none more important than my first time being invited to dinner at a white family's home. It was the same day I tried devil's vomit for the first time (also known as date loaf).

During my junior year of high school, I worked at a pet store in Scarsdale, New York, which was about an hour bus ride from my house. Like most of Westchester County, Scarsdale was very white. But unlike the other parts of lower Westchester County, it wasn't blue-collar middle-class white; it was wealthy upper-class white.

For context, Scarsdale was listed as the second-wealthiest

town in America in 2019, and Westchester County was among the wealthiest counties in the country when I was in high school.

Another distinctive factor about not only Scarsdale but wealthy parts of Westchester generally is that most of the white people there consider themselves politically and socially liberal. But they will still do and say problematic things. They either don't know or don't care that they are problematic.

I met a lot of these types of customers at the pet store. They'd come in and ask for my help finding things like dog food and then, after speaking with me, say something like "I'm happy you're doing something constructive with your time and not out in the streets. You should consider college." As if I weren't an honors student and would otherwise be spending my time robbing banks.

While these interactions made it hard to work there, I did become close with some of my white coworkers who were from the area, in particular two guys I'll call Patrick and Matt for the sake of anonymity and avoiding a lawsuit.

The two of them managed to get along with everyone. They also acted like their families didn't have a boatload of money, almost as if they were like the rest of us—working because we had to.

I would talk with them about everything—sports, video games, anime. It seemed like anything I was into, they were as well.

One day, we were on break, talking about the game Super Smash Bros. (which was my jam, and if you haven't played it, you've lived a lesser life), and Patrick suggested that Matt and I come over that Sunday to have dinner and play the game with him.

Up until that point, I'm not sure that I had ever been in a white person's home, which might sound surprising, but I didn't live near any white people, and the families of my white classmates weren't really the "invite the Black kid over" types.

I figured, "Hell, if people can go to the moon, I can try dinner with white people." Plus, I had seen enough episodes of *7th Heaven* and *Boy Meets World* to know what to expect. So I accepted the invite.

One small step for Frederick Joseph, one giant leap for Black kids with a couple of white friends everywhere.

I wasn't nervous about the dinner itself, but I was anxious about when it would be taking place. Sundays for me were a very sacred time, and I had a specific view of how they worked.

Growing up, I started and finished every Sunday the same way. I would wake up to the sound of my mother playing soul music and the smell of her cooking grits and canned salmon (we didn't have fresh-salmon money then), and I would have four minutes of peace in bed before she would yell, "Get up and do your chores!"

That was the routine for most of my life as a kid. I would get up on Sundays, eat breakfast, and then help clean our apartment while my mother cooked dinner, which typically included collard greens, corn bread, and mac and cheese.

> ⏸ You should know, I can basically taste the food while writing this. I know everyone says this, but my mother is legitimately the best cook. Her food isn't always healthy—and I have no problem throwing my mom under the bus about that—but it's good as hell.

But my house wasn't the only place like this on Sundays. You could smell similar scents at my cousin's house and hear the same types of soul music down the hall at my neighbor's house. This was how my mother was raised, and countless other Black people as well. If you weren't up cooking and cleaning, you were in church.

In fact, the music and the foods might have been different, but this was the same scene in the homes of many people of color around the country. Food, music, and family are the essence of race and culture for many of us.

I was actually pretty interested to find out what a "white Sunday" looked like. What did white people eat? What was the white version of soul music—the Beatles? Or maybe Elvis (who was a racist thief—google it if you don't believe me)?

The experience I ended up having at Patrick's house was not only void of everything I was used to, but it tainted my Sundays for the rest of time.

That Sunday afternoon, I arrived at Patrick's house in a cab and was immediately impressed. They lived in a home with a driveway gate that had a video intercom. This already put them in a higher class than the white television families I had seen.

After my cab was let past the gate, I saw that Matt's car was already there, which eased my mind; I wouldn't have to meet Patrick's family alone.

I rang the bell, and within seconds the door was opened by a tall white woman who looked like she could have been Tina Fey's sister. She stared at me for a moment, as if to take in what I was wearing and confirm that I wasn't a threat, and then said, "You must be Frederick. Come on in!"

I thanked her for having me and handed her a pie I had bought at Trader Joe's. I figured that would be the easiest thing to bring them, as everyone loves Trader Joe's, regardless of what race they are or how much money they have.

When I walked in, I was greeted by Patrick's father, who sort of reminded me of Ben Affleck. (Not the Batman version, the out-of-shape version.) He shook my hand and said, "It's a pleasure to meet you, son," then followed up with, "Strong handshake like that on a boy your size, I'm sure you can palm a basketball. You can probably dunk, too. No NBA in your future?"

■ You're probably thinking, *Wow, that was racist as hell.* You're right: it was. If you're not thinking this, we

have A LOT of work to do, and you should refer to the
stereotypes entry in this book's encyclopedia.

I didn't know how to respond, and luckily I didn't have
to, because at that moment, Patrick came downstairs to
greet me and take me upstairs to their game room. (Yes,
they were that rich.)

When we got to the room, Matt was sitting there playing *Smash Bros.* with Patrick's brother, who was about eleven
years old. After a few minutes of talking, I got comfortable
and joined them.

We played for a few hours, then Patrick's parents called
us downstairs for dinner, which surprised me because I
hadn't smelled any food being cooked.

When we got to the dining room, there were about ten
cartons of Chinese food laid out. As I said, I'd had no idea
what to expect from a white family dinner—maybe a green
bean casserole?—but it certainly wasn't Chinese takeout.

When Patrick's father went to turn on the radio, I figured I would at least get to hear what their Sunday music
was, but I was wrong. Instead, he turned on NPR (National
Public Radio), which I've come to realize is like religion for
liberal white people.

I suppose Patrick's parents could tell I was confused,
because they asked me what was wrong. I told them all
about Sundays in my household and about my mother's
cooking.

Patrick's mother responded by saying, "That sounds nice! What does your mother make?"

Before I could respond, Patrick's brother jumped in and said, "Fried chicken!" and laughed, assuming we'd all think his comment was funny.

Patrick's father swiftly turned to his youngest son and said, "That's not funny, Michael. Apologize to Frederick!"

But I jumped in with "It's okay." In fact, there was nothing okay about it, but I was so embarrassed and hurt that I just wanted to move past this deeply racist moment.

I was expecting one of my friends to stick up for me and condemn what was said, but Patrick simply chimed in by saying, "Michael, you're a little jerk," and then changed the conversation to how the Yankees were doing that season.

I sat quietly for the rest of dinner, picking at my food until everyone was done eating. After Patrick's parents cleared the table, his brother went back up to the game room, and his parents asked the three of us to stay downstairs for dessert and to talk.

We went into the den and Patrick's mother and father sat for a second and stared at me. Then Patrick's father said, "Frederick, I want to apologize to you."

At that point, I would rather have been anywhere in the world but in that room, surrounded by white people staring at me. Looking back, it felt like I was in the Sunken Place from *Get Out*.

So I simply said again, "It's okay," hoping I could just call a cab and head home soon.

Patrick's father slammed his hand on a table near him and said, "It's not okay! I don't know where he got that from!" Which was interesting, seeing as he was the same person who made the racist basketball comment when I walked in.

An older me would have said, "He obviously got it from you, Chad." But I said nothing.

⏮ I don't know if his name was Chad. I just figured he looked like a Chad, or maybe a Dan. I also imagined that he had played lacrosse and would shotgun beers at frat parties in college.

Patrick's mother said, "The reason we are frustrated by what Michael said is because in this family, we don't see color. When you are here, it doesn't matter if you're black, orange, or purple. You're a human, Frederick."

Both Patrick and Matt nodded and smiled at me when she was finished to affirm that they were on the same page as her. I just sat and stared at them, then stared around the room.

She then proceeded to go into the kitchen to get dessert.

There are two sayings that almost every person of color has heard various times in their life: "Why does everything have to be about race?" and "I don't see color."

These sayings are directly responsible for many of my

migraines over the years, and more important, they are part of the reason for a lack of racial progress in this country.

While I might not have been as thoughtful about racism when I was younger as I am now, I still hated the idea of people not seeing color, because it *doesn't make sense*. You can't tell me that you don't see my Blackness when you have to *see my Blackness* to even make the statement. The statement contradicts itself.

Beyond making no sense, the statement is also extremely racist, even though most people saying it think it's the exact opposite. But I wouldn't learn that until later in life.

When Patrick's mother walked back into the den, she was holding something that looked like banana bread, which I was happy about. The least they could do was have a solid dessert to end the night.

She cut everyone a piece, and they began eating. I picked up my piece and took a bite and quickly realized this wasn't banana bread at all. It wasn't sweet, and the texture was off.

I asked what it was, and Patrick's mother responded, "Date loaf." I didn't know what the hell date loaf was, nor did I care; I had had enough. First they ruined my Sunday dinner, then they were racist, and now they were trying to poison me!

> **❚❚** For those who aren't aware, date loaf is basically bread with nuts and dates. It can be camouflaged as other things, such as banana bread, and is disgusting.

It tastes like soggy wheat bread with crunchy nuts and fruit in it.

I don't know why anyone would eat it themselves or serve it to their guests, unless that person is pulling an elaborate prank—or hates their guests.

I got up and went to the bathroom and called my cab. When I was walking back to the den, Matt was standing there, and he asked whether I was okay. I told him I was getting ready to leave because Patrick's family was racist. He responded by telling me I was wrong and that they said they didn't see color.

I tried to explain why that didn't make sense, but he told me I was "looking for something to be mad about."

◀◀ While I'm paraphrasing a lot of conversations in this book, some of the things that were said I never forgot and remember word for word. That comment of Matt's is one of them.

A few minutes later, Patrick's father told me my cab was outside, and I thanked them and left.

I thought about the day the entire ride home, and then I thought about it the next day, and I kept thinking about it for months, and now years.

I didn't just think about the racist things that happened. I thought about how everyone had created a shield so I couldn't criticize their racism and how I also felt my Blackness being erased in the process. I disliked myself for a long time for giving them that power, for not holding them accountable.

I've come to realize that a fear of accountability is why white people say things like "I don't see color" and "Why does everything have to be about race?" Because to see my color, to see my culture, to see my race, would also mean taking responsibility for how white people have historically treated people my color, with my culture, from my race.

I may not have realized it when I was younger, but being at Patrick's house helped me come to terms with something important: from the expectations and stereotypes about what foods we eat to what talents we have or what activities we enjoy, every interaction in some way is influenced by race.

More important, talking about and combating racism doesn't "make everything about race"—*racism* makes everything about race, and racism can be found in every part of society. From our **educational system** to our legal system, nonwhite people are disproportionately mistreated and oppressed.

> **11** Except when it comes to food; I can safely say that green bean casserole is a form of white oppression.

AN INTERVIEW WITH ANGIE THOMAS

Producer, storyteller, and author of the best-selling book
The Hate U Give

Between conversations online and in professional settings, I've spent a lot of time discussing the reasons it's important that white people not only see race but also understand the active role their **color blindness** has played in racism. One of those discussions was with Angie Thomas.

One of my favorite things about Angie is how her work is authentically Black and relatable while holding white people and oppressive systems accountable.

ANGIE: Whenever I sit down and write, I never really sit down with an intention to talk about racism or with an intention to talk about issues that may be affecting young Black people. I just want to really tell stories about young Black people and the things they may experience, and in *The Hate U Give*, we see that with Starr. She experiences, of course, racism, police brutality, **systemic racism**. All of these things affect her life, affect her world. But for me, I wanted to simply tell a story about a Black girl in a community like Garden Heights and the struggle she had with being two different people in two different worlds.

This is an important point because it shows the inherent difference between the lives of many people of color and those of many white people. Angie didn't set out to write a book about racism or oppression; she set out to write a Black girl's story. But to tell most Black stories, it would be inauthentic not to include the racism impacting their world. This is another benefit of white privilege: white storytellers don't have to create characters or worlds that are impacted by things such as police brutality or systemic racism if they don't want to.

ANGIE: I hear white authors saying things all the time like "Oh, I just decided to make this character Black because it would be great to have that. But I'm not doing any research on Black people." You know what I mean? It's like you just took a white character and essentially gave them blackface, and no, it doesn't work like that. There are certain things, there are certain experiences, that Black characters are going to have that'll be different. So it's always good to take note of that. It's always good to be aware of that.

Let's say, for instance, if you were writing a story about time travel, and you were sending characters to the 1960s. It's going to be a whole different experience for a Black character than for a white character. You have to know these things. You have to be aware of these things.

In order to know these things, you need to first acknowledge that there is a difference. You need to see race. My experience at Patrick's house didn't happen because I'm "a human"; if so, it could have happened to Matt. But it didn't happen to him; it happened to me, because I was the Black person there.

ANGIE: I tell people, just say no to color blindness. I hate that phrase "I'm color-blind, I'm color-blind." I don't need you to be color-blind. I need you to see me as I am, I need you to see that I'm a Black woman. I need you to read my characters and see that they're young Black people. I need you to take note of that. I need you to recognize that, because it makes a difference. That's the world we live in. But when somebody says, "Oh, I'm color-blind," that also means they're purposely being blind to the things that affect me as a person of color.

In my opinion, the idea of being color-blind and of trying to steer conversations away from race are the most manipulative and powerful tools of racism. They allow white people to continue to be comfortable. No awkward conversations about race! No having to account for the centuries of brutality and injustice perpetrated by people who look like them against people who look like us!

But that color blindness doesn't help people of color who are in uncomfortable or downright dangerous situations every day because of race. And refusing to acknowledge race certainly doesn't save the lives of those who are killed because of it.

> ▶▶ Think I'm overstating the impact of color blindness? I suggest heading to the encyclopedia, my friend.

The inability of people to accept accountability for doing things that are wrong is in the DNA of America. It's why people can't accept that America was founded on land stolen from indigenous people and that Black people are still feeling the legacy of slavery.

I'm going to assume (hope) that you've heard of **Black Lives Matter**—the movement that started in the wake of the murder of Trayvon Martin, which seeks to draw attention to the disproportionate degree of police violence experienced by Black people in this country. You've probably *also* heard of **All Lives Matter**, which might seem like a fairly neutral statement but is actually anything but. (And then there's Blue Lives Matter—the movement to remind everyone that white killer cops are people, too.)

All Lives Matter is directly related to white people not wanting to see color and not wanting to make things about race. It's an effort to derail the people who are saying that Black lives matter while they are burying children like Trayvon Martin and Tamir Rice. It's an effort to neutralize the message that we need to uplift the importance of Black lives because so many people act as if those lives don't count.

I want you to see my race, and I want you to see the race of other people of color and the traumas many white people have caused us, and I want you to own those traumas and to be better.

But I also want you to see more than our pain and our struggle. I want you to see the beauty in our differences.

I want you to see Black mothers perfecting their collard greens recipe. I want you to see Chinese grandparents teaching their children to make dumplings by hand. I want you to see Puerto Rican fathers teaching their children the history of salsa music. I want you to see Indian mothers placing colorful saris on their daughters.

I don't want to be seen as "a human," I don't want to be seen as "the same." I want to be respected. I want to be special. I want to be jazz. I want to be soul food. I want to be poetry.

I want to be Black.

2

WE CAN ENJOY ED SHEERAN, BTS, AND CARDI B

Featuring Naima Cochrane and April Reign

I was in the cafeteria of my new high school, and someone started playing a Backstreet Boys song. Of course I went over and started singing along.

Keep in mind, boy bands were a staple of my childhood. You would've had to be from Antarctica to have never heard anything by the Backstreet Boys, NSYNC, and 98 Degrees.

> ⏭ 98 Degrees was actually the best of the boy bands, and I will gladly die on that hill. I've been making this point for years, and no one wants to listen. Go compare and see for yourself. Anyway, back to the story.

So there I was, in the middle of finally enjoying myself with all those white kids, but then someone cut me off in the middle of singing and said, "I didn't think you would know this song..."

"Why wouldn't I know the Backstreet Boys?"

He responded, "You know, you guys mainly listen to rap and stuff like that!"

There it was.

One of the things I remember most from high school is the idea of Oreos. Not the cookies—I've been very familiar with those amazing creations for as long as I can remember. No, I'm talking about the term "Oreo" as in the phrase "You're like an Oreo: Black on the outside and white on the inside."

I had never heard this term until I transferred to my new high school, and then I heard it A LOT.

I stood there, dumbfounded. Not only because I had never heard this stereotype before, but also because I couldn't believe he thought that was true. But I found out through the years that he wasn't the only white person who thought this way.

Since I was a kid, my interests have always been diverse and dynamic. I've always loved all types of movies, shows, books, and music. Most of the music I was introduced to was through my mother.

When I was growing up, my mother listened to everything. On any given day in my house you could hear the Bee Gees, Carole King, Fleetwood Mac, the Beatles, and more.

Because of this, I never saw certain genres or musicians as reserved for white people. It was the music I grew up hearing, along with DMX, Mary J. Blige, Marvin Gaye, Aretha Franklin, and Miles Davis.

But I learned during high school that liking things that weren't "Black" meant I was some type of special Black person. Like a mythical unicorn, or some sort of rare trading card that the white kids (and some of the white teachers) wanted to show off to people. Or a damn cookie.

If I knew a Fall Out Boy song, I was an Oreo. If I watched *One Tree Hill*, I was an Oreo. Hell, I couldn't even play certain video games without being called an Oreo.

It wasn't just the Black kids that were seen this way; it was anyone who wasn't white. If you didn't stick to things that white kids thought you should stick to, if you were different from what they assumed you should be, then odds were they would make fun of you for it.

The kids of color who weren't Black but who defied racial stereotypes were often called "golden Oreos." Tan on the outside, yet also white on the inside. Really clever, right? I'm sure kids in my high school kept Oreo's stock doing great.

As I look back, another reason I hate that white kids called us Oreos is because many white people hate, and I mean HATE, being referred to as foods.

If you call a white person "mayonnaise" or "mayo," many of them will lose it. But there is nothing more intense (or funnier, assuming you're at a safe distance) than seeing a white person lose their damn mind about being called a "cracker." I've literally seen white people argue that it is a direct parallel to a Black person being called the n-word. Which is obviously idiotic in many ways.

> ⏩ If you don't know why it's idiotic, you may need to skip to chapter 10 right now and learn about things you can't say.

It really wouldn't have mattered whether they called us Oreos or something nice like "unicorns" or "special," because none of it ever made sense. There wasn't anything different about me or the other kids who had these labels. Every person of color I knew was into all sorts of interesting and random things. Because they were individuals.

I remember sitting in class once and talking about the upcoming Star Wars movie with a friend. I was extremely excited because I was and am a huge fan, as is my mom, as is my uncle, and my younger brother, and most people in my family. The love for Chewbacca and Darth Vader has been passed down for generations.

As I was telling my friend about what I was hoping would happen in the new movie, my teacher overheard us and said, "You're a Star Wars fan?" I replied, "Yeah, I'm going to see it this weekend." He said, "Oh, that's surprising. I didn't know Black people liked Star Wars."

⏸ Now, this may not seem like an issue to many of you, but it's deeply problematic that a teacher would assume that someone wouldn't watch arguably the most popular movie series in history simply because they are Black. Not only does this assume that all Black people like or *dislike* the same things—another example of stereotyping, which you should have already read about!—but it also implies that the Star Wars movies are made specifically for white people. And that's just plain racist. And ignorant. (Funny how often those two things go hand in hand.)

Honestly, I can't recall how I ended up replying to that teacher or whether I did at all. But as I sit here, I wish I had gotten his racist ass fired. I remember his name, but he isn't worth the paper.

But where did this idea come from, that people of color could only like certain things? Growing up, I knew Black kids who were into anime, Asian kids who were into hip-hop, Latinx kids who were into theater, Arab kids who were into salsa, and so on. The people of color I knew were into all sorts of things. None of us was "special"—and none of us was any type of cookie. We were just ourselves.

I started understanding it as I got older. Some white people don't assume people of color to be dynamic or layered, because many white people have never had to be dynamic or layered themselves.

⏸ Now, I can already hear you white readers saying, "What are you talking about, Fred? I have all kinds of interests. I like Beyoncé! I'm layered!" And sure, maybe you like a variety of things. But how many of those things are from white culture? Most of them? All of them? If the majority of your interests are from a single culture, from the **mainstream** culture, then I hate to break it to you, but: you're not layered.

But it's not necessarily white people's fault that so many of them have a lack of awareness about other cultures. Many white people don't know any better.

A large part of white privilege is that it steers white people toward their cultural comfort zones. In countries like America, where most aspects of culture are controlled by white people, their culture has become the norm or mainstream.

In America, almost everything you can think of has been created to be comfortable and familiar for white people, and everything else is usually "other," "diverse," or "different."

Whether it's food, music, movies, clothes, or other aspects of culture, "the norm" is usually based on what white people know and enjoy. Like with anything, not stepping outside of what you're accustomed to creates a level of ignorance.

In the case of assuming that people of color can't or shouldn't be dynamic, and calling them things such as Oreos, it can also create a level of arrogance.

In a way, white privilege is actually part of the reason

that many people of color are so dynamic. Since much of mainstream culture is rooted in whiteness, we grow up learning, knowing, and even loving many things that aren't rooted in our culture.

For instance, there are very few people who haven't seen or don't know about the shows *Sex and the City* and *Friends*, two shows starring all-white casts with characters who have adventures, experiences, and privileges that most people of color simply can't relate to. So, then, why do we all know about these shows? Because they were everywhere, and still are.

Entertainment that centers white people and their experiences isn't just ingrained in American culture and values; it *is* American culture and values. So much so that Netflix spent $100 million to keep *Friends* on its platform in 2018. (If you've never seen the show, trust me, it's not worth nearly that.)

Around the same time that *Friends* and *Sex and the City* were on television, so were the shows *Living Single* and *Girlfriends*. They both had similar premises to the other two shows, except they had all-Black casts. Both are considered classics in the Black community.

But if you ask most white people if they've seen them, the answer is going to be no. Trust me, I know, because I've been asking white people for years, and I'm deeply annoyed almost every time I get an answer.

The issue isn't simply that white people haven't seen the shows; the issue is that they haven't even *heard* of them. Which says a lot about not only what entertainment is platformed but also the level of interest among white people in entertainment by people of color that doesn't have mainstream appeal, which again is another way of saying *white* appeal.

You can point to the same results with almost anything that has cultural or racial relevance. Music is possibly the best example, as most modern music has roots in music originated by people of color, and yet mainstream music is largely *white* music.

To prove my point, I ran a little experiment before writing this book.

I had a party, and I made sure the attendees were pretty diverse. It was basically the United Nations in my house: There were Black people, brown people, white people, Asians, Latinxs—we even had some representation from the Pacific Islands.

The goal was to make sure I was getting a wide spectrum of people to help prove the point of this chapter and make my case to all of you.

(For those of you who are thinking that I probably stacked the deck by choosing people who don't know a lot of music, or that I simply have friends who aren't very cultured, rest assured that I made sure to invite all of my friends who either work in the music industry or are musicians. These people are supposed to *know* music.)

As everyone arrived, I played top radio hits that I was sure people had heard, at least in passing, over the past few years. And I was right: Everyone either sang along, danced, or bopped familiarly to the various songs I played.

Now that they were warmed up, I told the group that we were going to test everyone's musical knowledge. Over the next hour, I played a random assortment of music from all different genres, time periods, and cultures. The one thing all of the songs had in common was that at one point or another they were very popular.

Whether it was Ariana Grande, the Jonas Brothers, Katy Perry, or Maroon 5, if the songs were mainstream hits by white artists, everyone in the room would say that they'd heard them before.

And not only did people in the room know the songs and the artists, for the most part they also knew deeper information about them, such as other songs of theirs, people the artists had dated, or when the artists had become popular.

Remember, it wasn't just the white people in the group who knew these things; it was everyone.

Well, except me. I personally don't care about how many people Ariana Grande has dated or how long her ponytail is. But it would seem that I'm in the minority on that.

The point is, across the board, people from various backgrounds had a great sense of who the artists were and what their music was all about. This didn't surprise me; as

I mentioned, everyone there was involved in music in one way or another.

Next, I decided to play songs that were extremely popular based on listens and views streaming but that weren't by white artists. This is where things got interesting.

I thought the first song should be easy, so I played "Ms. Jackson" by OutKast. As soon as the beat dropped, people started moving and then rapping along with the song. I knew I had picked the right song—until I looked at the white people in the group.

Of the six white people in the room, only one of them even seemed to know what was on. I was deeply confused. So I asked the other five white people if they knew the song. Not only did they not know the song; they didn't even know the *group*.

I almost passed out! I couldn't believe that they didn't know the song, let alone recognize the voices of André 3000 and Big Boi. OutKast was hardly some little-known group; they were actually one of the highest-selling groups of *all time*.

Their last album went diamond. I mean, as of this writing, only 122 albums have ever gone diamond. EVER!

After that, I needed a moment, so I gave the aux to other people at the party to see what people knew. We played all sorts of genres, from hip-hop to bachata, and generally all of the people of color had a familiarity with the music, even if it didn't belong to their culture. As I said before, knowing or liking things that are rooted in other communities has always been normal for the people of color that I know. But song after song, genre after genre, if it wasn't an artist or song that had crossed over into mainstream whiteness, my white guests didn't all know it.

Before everyone left, I decided to give the game one last try. First I played a few songs I was absolutely sure everyone in attendance would know.

I played "Livin' on a Prayer" by Bon Jovi, the quintessential white anthem. Every single person in the room sang along. I followed up with "Smells Like Teen Spirit" by Nirvana and "Don't Stop Believin'" by Journey, to the same results.

Everyone was singing along, and my house sounded like a crappy college bar.

Next, I played "Gasolina" by Daddy Yankee, and people started laughing, because that song is laughable. I expected to look around and see everyone singing along, but only two of the white people knew it.

For my final song I decided to play "Hot in Herre" (don't look at me; Nelly decided to spell it that way) by Nelly, and everyone knew it. I was wonderfully pleased that at least everyone knew one of Nelly's worst songs.

As people were preparing to leave, one of my friends said, "You can't have the last song of the night be one of those terrible Nelly songs." He wasn't wrong, so I jumped back on the aux and told everyone I was going to play another Nelly song. A second later I threw on "Flap Your Wings," a classic and a staple for many. Everyone was hyped. Well, *almost* everyone.

I looked at my white friends, and they looked confused. I asked one of them what was wrong. She said, "I thought you were going to play Nelly."

I stared at her for a second, then said, "This is Nelly playing right now." She said, "Oh, wow! Never heard it!"

I proceeded to kick everyone out immediately.

Maybe you're thinking that my white friends—who, let me remind you, *work in the music industry or are musicians themselves*—just happen to be unusually ignorant when it comes to music. But you'd be wrong. And my conversation with Naima Cochrane proves it.

AN INTERVIEW WITH NAIMA cOcHRANE

Career music-industry executive turned music historian and writer

Naima's musical knowledge and passion have garnered her a large social-media platform. Fun fact: she's named after the John Coltrane song "Naima," so you could say she was born into music.

> ❚❚ I'm sure many of you don't know who John Coltrane is, because life is unfair. I don't blame you, but go listen to "Naima" by Coltrane right now. Just know that if we

meet and you haven't listened to any Coltrane songs, we
are going to have an issue!

I figured she was the perfect person to ask about her
experiences in the industry, since she is a person of color
with varying interests in and knowledge about music and
entertainment that rival those of her white counterparts.

While she was growing up, Naima's parents played all
types of "Black music," so her understanding of the spectrum of what Black people supposedly did and didn't listen
to was shaped from a young age.

NAIMA: My parents were into the Nigerian singer Fela, jazz, and
Santana, in addition to soul and stuff like that. But they didn't necessarily listen to contemporary R&B aside from, like, Luther
[Vandross], and Janet [Jackson], and then Sade. I had a very global
understanding of my Blackness, not a super-defined and rigid
cultural understanding of my Blackness.

This was similar to my own musical upbringing, which
was very diverse and dynamic as well. Which is part of the
reason why, as a teenager, I didn't understand why so many
of the white people I met thought people of color enjoy only
certain things.

NAIMA: During elementary school and the first half of
middle school, I went to a predominantly white school, and

specifically a predominantly country white school. I was listening to the pop stations. I was listening to Guns N' Roses, and I was listening to the little bubble-gum pop music or whatever. In high school, I had to catch up on some of this early hip-hop. I had to catch up on Salt-N-Pepa. I had to catch up on the first N.W.A. album.

Because of how I grew up, during my career, I didn't just have opinions on the Black music. I had opinions on the alternative music, and the white music, and the straight-up pop music, and informed opinions, since I could tell you if I liked it or if I didn't like it, and why. It made me a better marketer, because I was pulling from broader experience. I remember we were doing something for Foster the People when I was at Columbia, and I mentioned something about Hacky Sack because I remember watching kids at school play Hacky Sack. The band members were surprised, because they figured that's not a reference that a lot of Black kids are going to throw out, or that a lot of Black people are going to throw out.

While it has always bothered me how many white people view people of color and our ability to be dynamic, it actually confuses me when it comes to Black people and music. As I said earlier, most popular music in America is rooted in Black music and culture—a point that Naima addressed at length.

NAIMA: Well, first of all, from a historical standpoint, Black music is the foundation for so many other genres of music. Or if not Black music being the foundation, Black artists inspired trends. Black music, rhythm and blues, true rhythm and blues, and some gospel is the basis for country western.

If you take the lyrics from country songs and just change a couple of little things, change it from a truck to a Cadillac or something, and put it under a different beat, it's an R&B song, right? And there is a Black woman, Loretta Thorpe, who inspired some huge country and rock and roll guitarists. So there's that. Gospel and blues also served to inspire, obviously, rock and roll. Ike Turner is credited by most people for having the first rock and roll song. And jazz is the basis for so many other art forms. It's the basis for electronic, and techno, and house. So much is built off of things that were pioneered during the jazz era. So I just think that our music, our rhythm, our syncopation, our different use of style, call and response—all of that comes from Black people.

Black music is the foundation of American music, period. We created this sh*t, basically.

I may get that last line on a T-shirt. "We created this sh*t, basically." Preach, pastor Naima!

Naima next spoke about her experiences in the music industry, which weren't all that different from my experiences at the party I hosted to make my point for this chapter—the one in which I had to kick everyone out because of that Nelly nonsense.

NAIMA: So, you mentioned earlier that Black people often make better marketers because we have to be aware of everything, right? We can't just know our own sh*t. We also have to know the mainstream stuff in pop culture, in marketing trends, in retail—whatever area we work in, we still have to know. So, even if I worked in urban marketing, if I don't know what the top ten are—all Top 10 songs on the Hot 100—they're going to look at me like I'm crazy. But nobody who is white and works in the pop department has to know all ten songs on the Hot R&B and rap charts. They don't have to know that, but I need to know everything that's on the Hot 100 and Top 40 chart. Right? So there's always been that double standard that I don't even think white people are aware of culturally. And I've tried to bring that to people's attention.

In my career, it's been surprising to some people how much I can speak to. I kind of like catching people off guard like that. There was a time when I had a [white] boss with me at an industry event and they played "Before I Let Go," and he was like, "How does everybody know this song?"

◀◀ You may have heard the cover of "Before I Let Go" because Beyoncé released it with her *Homecoming* docufilm. SHE IS NOT THE ORIGINATOR OF THIS SONG! Black people have been listening to it for decades. It's by Frankie Beverly and Maze, and they have many other amazing songs. If you haven't heard it, go listen. That is all; back to our scheduled programming.

NAIMA: And I was like, "This is ... Every Black person in America knows this song." Every Black person in the world might know this song. This was like the unofficial Black national anthem. He had no idea who Frankie Beverly and Maze was; he had never heard the song before.

And when, you know, the DJ cuts the music out so everybody can go [singing], his mind was blown, because it was literally everybody in the whole entire space.

We started singing the song lightly and laughing on the phone.

NAIMA: And I was like, "This is us. We would know 'Sweet Caroline.' We would know 'Sweet Home Alabama.' We would know the Joints. But you guys don't know 'Before I Let Go.'" I've tried to use my position to educate where I can. It takes some patience, and not everybody has the patience to do that.

Just as Naima and I had had similar experiences with white people in the music industry, we also had had similar experiences in high school as kids who defied our racial stereotypes.

NAIMA: So I definitely got called, like, a white girl, and you know, I was kind of clowned a little bit because I had to play some catch-up based on where I grew up. The thing is, Blackness is not a monolith, and the same can be said about other cultures. This is why it's so important for young people to understand that they can be whoever they want, like whatever they want, and do whatever they want. Either way, you're still you. Black, brown, white, whatever.

Of all the points Naima made, this point was probably the most important to me, because it speaks directly to the idea that people are who they are, and that shouldn't alter their validity in their community. It's important not only for white people to see that people of color exist in various ways; it's also important for people of color to see themselves that way. To understand that you can listen to whatever you want, watch whatever you want, be whoever you want, and become whoever you want. This is why people support movements such as **#RepresentationMatters**.

That's part of the reason I decided to also talk with my good friend April Reign.

AN INTERVIEW WITH APRIL REIGN

Diversity and inclusion advocate and founder of the
#OscarsSoWhite movement

April's efforts to diversify the Academy Awards and Hollywood as a whole have been praised by celebrities such as Gabrielle Union, Spike Lee, Reagan Gomez, and Kamau Bell, among others. The movement has been directly credited by many as helping to usher in a new era of diversity and inclusion in Hollywood by holding the industry accountable for a lack of both.

Needless to say, April is a powerhouse, but she is also just dope as hell and has important things to say, particularly when it comes to people of color being seen as dynamic. Starting with herself.

APRIL: I think I have always been drawn to art in various ways. I say that, acknowledging the fact that my stick figures are horrible, so there's no visual representation of that. I tried high school musical a couple of times, and that was horrible. I played the flute, and I was decent at that, and I was in band for a few years. But I have an immense amount of respect for people who can take something that sort of wells up and overflows within them and share that with the world. I'm always incredibly appreciative and respectful of people who are willing to be that open with strangers.

I think I'm one of the eight Black people who actually are fans of the Dave Matthews Band. Like, I truly do like DMB, have been to more than one concert. But I think that's also a product of being a military kid. My dad was in the army, so we moved around a lot. And so, that meant that I was exposed to a lot of music and entertainment because of the different locations.

⏸ She is correct. She is one of the eight Black people on this planet who enjoy the Dave Matthews Band. She is also the only one who tries to make "DMB" a thing. You know how I've been telling you to go check out certain movies and music being mentioned throughout the book? Yeah, this isn't one of those times.

I asked April what made her decide to call out the need for more representation in Hollywood through her digital movement.

APRIL: I believe that I was at the right place at the right time. I don't let them give me too much credit for that because I truly acknowledge that I stand on the shoulders of so many artists and activists or artivists, whatever, who have been saying the same thing that I was saying for years. Harry Belafonte and Ossie Davis and Ruby Dee and so many people were talking about the lack of representation of Black folks in film. I just had the opportunity to say basically the same thing, but on a newer platform.

I think when I created #OscarsSoWhite—this was January 2015—I had maybe eight thousand followers. So it wasn't the huge platform that I have now. And I think it resonated with people, but to be honest, #OscarsSoWhite didn't really take off until the following year, 2016, because that was the second year in which there were no people of color nominated for any of the acting categories at the best actor/actress or best supporting actor/actress levels. That means there were twenty slots that went to white folks.

I think people were taking it as, Okay, first time is a fluke; the second time is a pattern. And it was, Okay maybe this woman has something here.

In my opinion, many industries are entering a moment where they are being held accountable for their lack of space for and investment in people of color, and a lot of it is starting with young people. Many generations have added seats to the table, and I think younger generations now are focused on creating tables, which April spoke to as well. I believe #OscarsSoWhite is an example of why that is happening.

APRIL: I think part of #OscarsSoWhite's staying power is that everybody's talking about diversity and inclusion. And it's not just with respect to entertainment. It's also journalism. It's also tech. No industry is not touched by the fact that the more diverse your workforce is, the more money you make. It's statistically proven.

We may not agree on the merits of the Dave Matthews Band, but one thing we can both agree on is the greatness that is Star Wars. (That's right, high-school-teacher-whose-name-isn't-worth-printing-in-this-book, OTHER Black people like Star Wars, too!)

APRIL: I think the first movie that I recall seeing in a theater was *Star Wars*, what we now know as *Episode IV, A New Hope*. And I was seven at the time. That was 1977. Oh yeah, I've always been interested in a wide range of films. If it moves me, I'm interested in it. I don't like doing labels for myself. So I definitely don't like doing it for the entertainment I consume.

Because I don't like labels, I don't think that I ascribe to them. I like what I like. ... It's just never been an issue for me about labeling something that I've liked and didn't like and what it meant or anything. I think I had the privilege to not have to be put into a particular silo with respect to the kind of stuff I liked. It wasn't always what people refer to as Black films or whatever. If I were to list my top five films, *Godfather* one and two (we don't speak of three) would be in that group. And the one time that they referenced Black people in either of those films, they were using the word "nigger."

◼ Before I continue, I have to address something. In this book, the n-word comes up a few times. I was asked whether I wanted to censor it, or write "n-word," since the book is intended for a white audience, who shouldn't be saying that word. But that isn't authentic. So I will say this: if you're not Black, don't say it. Just because it's in the book, that doesn't mean you can read it aloud. Thanks!

APRIL: I think it's crucial that kids at a young age see themselves presented in a variety of ways. And even more so for marginalized kids. And when I say "marginalized" for this conversation, I'm talking about all of the categories that I talked about with #OscarsSoWhite, so not just race but also sexual orientation and gender identity and disability and ethnicity.

One of the first times that I've recognized Blackness as being something special was seeing Roosevelt Franklin on *Sesame Street*. Even though the Muppet itself was purple, you could tell that this was representing a Black kid, a Black kid with a single mom from the projects.

I think that's why shows like *The Cosby Show*, putting all of the sh*t with Bill Cosby aside, but shows like *The Cosby Show* were important, because they showed a family who had, for some people, "made it." The father's a doctor; the mother's a lawyer. They're upper middle class. They don't appear to want for anything. And then I think Cosby did a good job as Dr. Huxtable—there was that one episode with Theo and the Monopoly money. He's like, "*We're* rich. *You* don't have anything, Theo."

April is referring to the pilot episode of *The Cosby Show*. In that episode, one of the children in the family, Theo, thinks he doesn't have to do well in school or get a good job because his parents are well off. His father, played by Bill Cosby, teaches him a life lesson about the fact that he still needs to go out and make something of himself. There is an underlying message that it's that much more important for Theo to work hard because he's Black.

These types of lessons carried on throughout the eight years that *The Cosby Show* ran. In fact, social scientists were brought on to make sure the show didn't feed into any negative stereotypes about Black people. *The Cosby Show* also led to the highly successful spin-off sitcom *A Different World*, which was about Denise, one of the Cosby daughters, attending an **HBCU** (Historically Black College or University) during its first season.

While Bill Cosby is a piece of garbage, no one can deny that both *The Cosby Show* and *A Different World* were crowning achievements and guidelines not only for Black representation but for how people of color could be represented as a whole.

If you haven't seen either show, I suggest you do.

April had more to say about the importance of representation from a broad standpoint and how it helps people of color.

APRIL: So it's just like the movie *Coco*, how important it is for Latinx kids to see a vibrant kid who wants to be an artist, who also wants to support and be respectful of the family, but needs to live his truth. How fantastic is it that there are really young kids who are able to see that early on? And I think that's especially important for kids who are growing up knowing that they are going to have some challenges because of their sexual orientation or gender identity.

This is why movements such as #OscarsSoWhite, films like **Black Panther**, and artists like Lil Nas X are so important. They offer the ability for people to be seen in authentic ways that aren't simply the manifestation of how someone else has stereotyped them.

April ended our conversation with a few final thoughts on bigotry and privilege:

APRIL: I think that racism is learned, right? And we've seen that. Racism, unfortunately, or thoughts of bigotry and prejudice and so on, start in the home. And so ... if you've got your father or mother or caregiver who is deeply ensconced in bigotry and discrimination, and that's all you get, then hopefully this book will help show that there is another side.

When's the last time you've had a person of a different ethnicity or a different sexual orientation in your home? To study or just to play PS4 or what have you?

These last questions resonated deeply with me, because that's why I wrote this book and, I hope, why you're reading this. I want us to be more complete people. That starts with dropping our assumptions about a person. It starts with learning their stories.

And most important? It starts with Nabisco compensating me and millions of others who have been tormented because of Oreos.

3

CERTAIN THINGS ARE RACIST, EVEN IF YOU DON'T KNOW IT

Featuring Africa Miranda and Rabia Chaudry

Growing up, I was one of those kids who always had their head in a book. You know, the type of ten-year-old who reads encyclopedias and watches documentaries for fun.

I loved learning new things. I also loved that learning kept me distracted from the fact that I didn't have many friends.

> ⏪ Sad, I know. But don't worry, for better or worse, I became popular in high school. I also was no longer bullied. (Growing to over six feet and having my acne clear up helped.)

Because I was a walking *Encyclopedia Britannica*, I was placed in advanced courses, and in second grade it was recommended that I transfer to an honors school, though I decided not to leave my school, because I was nervous. My logic was that the bullies you know are better than the ones you don't, and I had been bullied long enough to know who was who.

II I realized while typing this that if you were born after 2000, you probably have no idea what the *Encyclopedia Britannica* is. Basically, before there was Google, there was software on discs that had information about specific subjects, such as dinosaurs. And rumor has it that before this information was on discs, it was in actual books—though that might just be an urban legend.

Whether you accessed the encyclopedias in book form or on discs, the point was that the information available didn't change. At least, not until the next edition, which sometimes could take YEARS. Don't worry, one day you'll be explaining what text messages are when people are talking over holograms.

While my school wasn't an honors school, it did have some very intelligent students. But based on the honor roll posted in the hallway every quarter (this must have been hell for some kids), no one could deny that I was one of the school's brightest.

I say "one of" because during that time I had a rival named Fatimah Martinez, who typically had the same exact grades as me. While I wouldn't say this when I was younger,

I'm a big enough person now to begrudgingly admit that she was just about as smart as me.

During those years, I wasn't one of the first kids picked for sports, asked to attend birthday parties, or sought out at lunch tables. But while socializing with other kids was hard, everything else about school couldn't have been easier.

Because of my interest in academics, many teachers were very kind to me. I think they also saw I didn't have many friends, so some would let me hang out during lunch and recess so I wouldn't have to be with other kids. (Yeah, it was that bad.)

At times I'd even get a chance to help them grade papers or prepare lessons. I was what some might call a teacher's pet, but I'd consider myself a survivor.

One of those teachers was Ms. Meyers, who always seemed to be my biggest supporter. Which is why I was disappointed when our class found out she was having a baby and we'd have a substitute for the rest of the year.

When the new teacher started, I was nervous, but I figured I had nothing to worry about as long as I kept excelling. As the good grades poured in, so would the love. It was simple.

On the substitute's first day, she took attendance and asked everyone to say "something interesting" about themselves.

> ⏩ You'll find out soon why I won't even dignify her with a fictional name. To help you visualize her, the substitute was an older white woman who looked like she dyed her hair to look younger, but the wrinkles told no lies.

When she got to my name, I took a second to respond because I was nervous one of the kids would say something "interesting" about me that would hurt my feelings. It wouldn't have been the first time.

Before I could find the courage to respond, she looked at a group of my white classmates and said, "I'm sure one of you is Frederick. Speak up."

So I said, "Sorry, I'm Frederick."

She turned to me and said, "Stop joking, please." Then she scanned her list and said, "Let me guess, you're Jamal."

I stared at her blankly and told her my name again. "I'm not joking, I'm Frederick Joseph."

> ⏪ I'm hoping that the last chapter made it clear why the sub's assumption about my name was racist as hell. If I had a time machine, I'd go back to the past and put a tack on her seat.

The actual Jamal was absent that day, but this one white kid (I'm not giving him a name, either) who hated me spoke up at that point, and though he reaffirmed that my name was, in fact, Frederick, he also let her and the rest of the class know that I was a "dork."

The substitute didn't apologize for the name mistake, nor did she apologize for letting the wolves publicly eat me alive. Little did I know, getting an apology from her would soon be the least of my concerns.

Over the next few days, I quickly learned that my life with the substitute was going to be completely different from my life with Ms. Meyers. No longer was I being called on to answer questions when I raised my hand or asked to help grade papers. But it wasn't just me; other kids of color were being treated differently now as well, including my rival, Fatimah. The substitute was paying much more attention to the white kids in class and making sure they participated.

But I knew that if there was anything that could win over the substitute, it was going to be my great test scores, and lucky for me we had a test coming up.

Unlike most students, test days were my favorite days. It was kind of like going into the NBA playoffs, but with a team that I knew was just better than all of the other teams. I also knew that ultimately I would end up competing only with Fatimah for best grade on the exam.

Because we typically both got the same grade (a perfect score, of course), we began competing in other ways on test days. We silently decided to start seeing who would finish their test first, because it wasn't enough just to be smart; you had to also be fast.

For our first test with the substitute I was going to bring my A game. She was going to learn just how good I was, and everything would be back to normal. The day of the test I was fully prepared (as always) and had even spent extra time reviewing my homework notes the night before.

As the substitute handed out the test, Fatimah looked at me menacingly, almost as if to let me know that she, too, would be bringing it, and I was excited. This was the Magic versus Bird of elementary school rivalries.

> ⏭ I just realized that many of you likely don't know who Magic Johnson and Larry Bird are, and that hurts me more than I can explain. They were two basketball players in the '80s and '90s and part of the reason Celtics and Lakers fans hate each other. (Let's go, Lakers.) Google.

Once we started the test, I was locked in. I only put my head up a few times to see how Fatimah was doing, and I caught glimpses of her doing the same to me. After about fifteen minutes or so, both Fatimah and I finished and darted to the substitute's desk to hand our tests in at basically the same time. (I won.)

Fatimah and I sat at our desks for the rest of the time and watched as our classmates finished their exams. Per usual on test day, we both had big smiles on our faces as we were leaving the class.

Before we walked out the door, the substitute stopped both of us and said she wanted to speak with us.

Once all of the other students were off to lunch, the substitute closed the door, then looked at us and said, "I know you two cheated."

I didn't know what to say, and by Fatimah's silence, I'm guessing she didn't, either. Eventually I spoke up and simply said, "No, we didn't."

The substitute responded by saying, "I saw you two looking at each other and cheating."

To which Fatimah responded, "We weren't cheating. We were just seeing if the other person was done. We were racing."

The substitute then said, "I graded both of your tests after you finished, and you both got a perfect score. It also looks like you've both been getting perfect scores on tests almost all year."

"Because we're both really smart," responded Fatimah.

"Or you're both really good at cheating. You're both articulate and do good work for students from your backgrounds"—yes, she really said this—"but none of the other students are getting these grades. So you'll both have to retake the test in front of me during recess to prove you haven't been cheating, or we can bring this to the principal."

Neither Fatimah nor I responded. We both went to lunch and came back to the classroom during recess to retake our test.

As the substitute placed the exams on our desks and told us to begin, I just sat there, confused about what her saying "from your backgrounds" meant. What made me and Fatimah different from the other kids?

Then I realized that Fatimah and I weren't just the smartest kids in the class; we were the only two nonwhite kids who were getting these types of grades. And the only way the substitute could make sense of that was to assume we were cheating. I was so distracted and disturbed by that idea that I couldn't concentrate on the test. By the time the substitute said we had ten minutes to finish the exam, I had to rush through it.

The substitute graded the two tests in front of us. Fatimah got a 78 percent and I got a 70 percent. (Yes, I remember the exact scores; the moment is etched in my brain.) Not bad for taking our second test of the day and having our intelligence questioned by a racist adult. But the substitute used it as confirmation that we had been cheating all year.

She looked at us, then looked down at our new grades, and then back up at us, and said, "This is why you don't cheat. You obviously both need to study more if you want to really be the best in your class. Think about how unfair it is to the other students who are actually getting better grades than you." (The white kids, she meant.) "You can be the ones to get your families out of your neighborhoods, but not if you're cheating yourselves."

Fatimah and I said nothing.

When I went home, I didn't tell my mother about what had taken place. When I eventually gave her my test, she was surprised by the grade and asked what had happened. I simply told her it was hard and left it at that.

In my mind, there was nothing to report back to my mother. She had taught me what blatant racism was in terms of things like the word "nigger." The substitute hadn't done anything that ten-year-old me could identify as racist, yet I felt it all the same. After that day, the substitute sat the two of us far enough apart that not only could we not "cheat," but we also couldn't interact.

I was so traumatized by the incident that I made sure not to get perfect grades on exams for the rest of the year to avoid having to deal with a similar incident.

I can't say whether Fatimah did the same, but her grades dropped as well. We were both still seen as good students, but we were no longer top in our class.

I wish I could say things got better after that year, when Fatimah and I moved on to a different grade with a different teacher. But the truth is, I've spent most of my life meeting people who were just like that substitute.

These were the white girls in high school who thought they were complimenting me by saying I was "cute for a Black guy"; the white guys who were apologetic that their parents wouldn't let them invite me to their house parties because "kids from the ghetto are thugs"; the older white lady at my pet store job who would tell me how "articulate"

I was; and the first boss I had after college, telling me I had "great taste in suits for someone from where I was from."

I spent years carrying the weight of all of those people who wouldn't let me just be great, the people who qualified the good and bad things about me by my race. If I was great, it was *for someone like me*, and if I failed, it was because I was *someone like me*.

The worst part is that it's difficult to call many of these people out, because they don't think they're being racist. Society has conditioned us to view people of color in negative ways. Which makes it more difficult to stop racist behavior, because people are often saying things based on assumptions from what they've been taught.

If the president of the United States (I'm referring to Trump) and the media consistently call Mexicans dangerous, rapists, and thieves, for example, a person hearing this could assume it's true and therefore expect every Mexican to be dangerous, a rapist, or a thief. So any Mexican they find to be an upstanding person is now the exception rather than the rule.

While these sorts of assumptions are inherently racist, it can be hard to get even well-meaning white people to see them this way. And damn near impossible to get white people who *don't* mean well to see them this way. And I get it. This stuff's complicated—which, I'm guessing, is why you're reading this book.

AN INTERVIEW WITH AFRIcA MIRANDA

Author, host, and digital personality
(I know, I keep some pretty dope people around me.)

I spoke with my friend Africa Miranda about people saying things and making assumptions that are subtly racist and how those internalized ideas impact not only people of color but white people as well.

AFRICA: One of the things, I think, is not even so much specific phrasing as it is just the surprise in their voices at times... When you get in these rooms with white people, their level of surprise that you either can match their experiences or supersede them is, like—it almost turns into a little dance where they'll kind of just throw things out that are very commonplace to them, be it the places that they travel or food.

It's like their markers of class, and those different things are food, travel destinations, sometimes clothing, but usually it's books that they've read or things they reference. I was on a reality show on Bravo and made some offhand reference to Miss Havisham from *Great Expectations*, and someone there had an awed reaction to me knowing about it. I'm thinking to myself, *Well, I have an English degree, I grew up reading every type of book.*

⏸ I had no clue who Miss Havisham was, because we didn't read *Great Expectations* in school. I went to google her, and the first few sentences bored me so much I decided I didn't need to know at this point. I'll let Africa and her white colleagues have that one.

AFRICA: I always go back to that Chris Rock special where he's, like, "What are we supposed to sound like?" You know what I mean? It's, like, "What did you think we were going to sound like, or should sound like? These are words. I'm not supposed to be able to string a sentence together?" You know, and it's not a compliment, and again, they're so surprised that you're so put together, and it's exhausting.

What I realized was that the more well spoken I was, the more polished I was, the more put together I was, it went from white people's surprise to their disdain, because as much as they think they like a well-spoken Black person, you go from the well-spoken negro to the uppity negro very quick, and what they don't like is a Black woman that is too free, too well spoken, too this, too that.

For many people, whiteness is the standard for intelligence, class, and talent. Which is why, as an example, if you're a person of color and you're articulate, some will say you "speak white."

It's why that substitute teacher couldn't fathom that a

young Latinx girl and a Black boy could be the most intelligent people in their class.

Often when white people find themselves in situations where people of color are simply better at something, they become resentful and sometimes even dangerous.

I learned over the years that behaviors like the ones Africa and I described and the traumas we've faced are **microaggressions** (which can at times scale to aggression; the case of that substitute is an example). I've spent years growing out of how I internalized the things people have said to me, and the assumptions they've made about people like me.

White privilege and power can take on many shapes, one of which is simply the opportunity to be seen as an individual with your own interests and lived experience.

Some white people come from low-income communities, some are thieves, some are uneducated, some play sports, some are articulate, some are good people, and some are trying to be. But no one assumes, just because some white people are thieves or are uneducated, that most if not all white people share these traits, and that those who don't are the exceptions.

To have someone judge you by getting to know you is a powerful and life-changing thing when you've never been treated that way.

Too often people of color are not treated as people at all but rather as ideas: the sum of what people have assumed and the little they've seen in passing. It's not only unfair; it is deeply racist and can be extremely detrimental. This dehumanization is part of why people have been enslaved and why people are killed by trigger-happy police officers.

Which is something I discussed with Rabia Chaudry.

AN INTERVIEW WITH RABIA cHAUDRY

Lawyer, author, and podcast host

I asked Rabia about the importance of white people getting to know people of color and spending time around them.

RABIA: Research has shown the benefits, and it's so scary because we talk about how in this postfactual era, the facts don't matter. Facts almost never change a person's mind. So you can provide all the data you want to somebody. They might have this horrible opinion about a group of people, and you can show them all the data you want, all the empirical evidence. It's not going to change their mind, but there's only one thing that will, and that is actually having a positive interaction with somebody of that group. It can literally be just one person they know from that group, which will make them resilient enough to say to someone making a bigoted comment, "I don't agree."

That personal interaction is one of the most powerful things to prevent people from falling into adopting really radical or bigoted or biased discriminatory views. That's really hard to do, though. It's hard to do. For me as a mother, my eldest, who's almost eleven now, she also goes to Islamic school. She goes to a Muslim school. But the way I live my life, my life is very inclusive. My social circle is very broad. It includes people of every religion, every sexual orientation, and I expose my kids to culture and music, and I want them to be global citizens.

I stuck to the Muslim schools because the last thing kids need at school is to be scared of people harassing them for their identity. They should go there, feel comfortable so they can study and learn and grow. That's why I decided to do that. But I have to make up for the fact that they are in these little bubbles in the Islamic school. Their world is not going to be just Muslims. The way we live, it helps, hopefully, to fill out the rest of those spaces.

Let's talk for a minute about bubbles. We all live in some sort of bubble, whether of race, gender, sexuality, religion, or other aspects of our identities or lived experience. Bubbles aren't inherently bad. Many people create their own bubbles to feel safe within a community of people with identities similar to theirs. For people like myself, bubbles can also help us learn more about ourselves, by being around people who appreciate the things we do.

But bubbles can also be dangerous, especially when people are forced into them or don't realize they are in them.

We've all been conditioned in our ignorance; no one can say that they don't make assumptions about people. The difference in white people making and verbalizing those assumptions is that in our society, white people often exist with privilege and power in spaces that people of color don't.

In the example of Fatimah and me, that substitute teacher's assumptions made her act in ways that had a long-lasting impact on two people of color and, frankly, could have derailed our lives. She had specific ideas about how kids who looked like me and Fatimah should perform in the classroom, and she was determined to put us in those little bubbles.

What if I'd believed her and lost the drive to ace those exams that people "like me" weren't supposed to ace? What if I had just believed all of the people who have called me a thug or said Black people are from the ghetto, and those who essentially told me that the white race is more attractive than my own?

This is how systemic racism works. It's not just a matter of blatant racism; it's also about conditioning people to think less of themselves.

> ⏸ As I write this, I'm thinking I should be calculating how much the government owes people of color for therapy costs.

We're not an assumption, we're not words like "thug," we're not a statistic, we're not a part of your imagination, and we are certainly not to be held to **white standards**.

We are the Black boy in class who happens to be from a low-income area who is also the smartest person in class (with Fatimah). We are our mistakes, we are our wins, we are good at things, and we are bad at things.

We are people, and we should be treated as such.

4

YOU COULD AT LEAST TRY TO PRONOUNCE MY NAME CORRECTLY

Featuring Xorje Olivares and Toni Adenle (Toni Tone)

"DayVaughn? DuhVon? DayVon? I'm sorry, I just can't pronounce this. Can someone give me a hand here?"

Whether it's a Black name, a Spanish name, an Asian name, or anything else, we've all seen this scene before: a white person trying to pronounce names that aren't white and acting like they are reading Elvish (a language from *Lord of the Rings*; I already told you I'm a nerd).

You know what group's names are actually difficult?

◼ I want you to take a moment and think about this.

It's a trick question. The answer is every group. All names are difficult because they are all made up!

Think about it. What makes a last name like Zuckerberg any less complicated than Henriquez or Shakur? The answer is simple: one is rooted in white standards, while the others are not. The same could be said for food, music, clothing, or any other aspect of culture that doesn't originate in white culture.

As I mentioned once or twice (maybe a billion times), my high school was much whiter than I was used to. My middle school, however, was predominantly Black, though many of the white kids were still very popular—and very problematic. While I definitely dealt with my fair share of ignorance and life-long traumatic memories (thanks again for reading about these), there are a few things I never went through.

For instance, I don't think anyone has ever had trouble pronouncing my name, because it's common in America and Europe, so it's been normalized. I will say, I used to hate when kids would call me Frederick Douglass to make fun of me, but it's been smooth sailing otherwise.

⏭ Shout-out to Frederick Douglass; I'd be honored if someone said that now. If you don't know who Mr. Douglass is, I suggest you throw your entire school system away—and also go online and learn more about him.

I didn't have anything about me culturally that they could deem weird or make fun of. Instead, as you know, they made fun of the fact that a lot of my tastes were actually mainstream—meaning white.

There were a few students who got it bad from both teachers and classmates. One person who comes to mind from middle school was my friend Karishma Patel, a young Hindu girl who for a long time flew under the radar.

I mean, teachers would absolutely butcher her name all the time, but otherwise she went unbothered—until she didn't.

Before I start this story, what you need to understand is that before there was social media, before there was text messaging, before there was the Internet, there was the school cafeteria.

I know cafeterias still exist, but imagine a world where there were no phones, and people had no choice but to interact while they had lunch.

If you needed information, if you needed to talk to someone, if a fight was going to break out, it was going to happen in the cafeteria.

For some, the cafeteria was a social utopia, while for others, it was an anxiety-inducing hell. At that point in my life, what it was for me depended upon the day.

My strategy was always to stay low and out of sight during lunch. Grab my tray, grab a drink, smile at the lunch lady who always gave me an extra boneless rib, get some fruit snacks, and head out.

This wasn't just my strategy; it was one passed down by

generations of unpopular students. It was the same strategy that Karishma used. But she was lucky; she had cultural food restrictions, so her parents sent her with food from home every day, which meant that she got to go straight to the safe zone during lunch.

⏮ Sorry, I should explain what the safe zone was. Basically, it was a haven for the outcasts. A table in the back of the cafeteria unofficially reserved for those of us who needed refuge from the potential horrors of lunchtime social interactions.

If you played Dungeons & Dragons, you would go to the safe zone. If you wore unfashionable hand-me-down clothes from your siblings, you would go to the safe zone. If you used to be popular but you had an "accident" in school, you would go to the safe zone. "Give me your tired, your poor, your nerdy-and-still-growing-into-their-looks masses yearning to breathe free..."

Because of the makeup of the people who sat at the table, there was never much discussion about race or culture. We were all more focused on our core similarity of being bullied outcasts and surviving than we were on the ways we weren't similar. Everyone was generally accepted for who they were.

One day, two of the kids at the table decided to have a light-saber duel. (YES, it was that nerdy.) Normally this wouldn't have been a problem. We could typically do what-ever we wanted, and no one bothered us, almost as if they couldn't see us.

Our own little middle-school Wakanda.

In the middle of dueling, one of the kids took it a bit too far and slapped the light saber out of the other kid's hand, and it went flying beyond our barriers.

◄◄ I'm probably making this up, but I swear I remember this all happening in slow motion and someone saying "Noooooo" as it was spinning in the air.

The light saber not only landed at one of the most popular tables, but it hit two of the most popular girls in school. Time stood still for a second before a group of girls sprang up from the table and marched toward us.

All of the girls looked exactly like the main girls in the movie *Mean Girls*: super fashionable, a lot of makeup, and very white.

►►I I know I do this every chapter, but if you haven't seen *Mean Girls*, just google it to get a picture of what I'm talking about.

As soon as they got to the table, one of them threw the light saber down and demanded, "Who threw this?"

The kid who'd knocked the light saber away responded, "I'm sorry—it was an accident."

The same girl responded swiftly and viciously by saying, "You look like *you* were an accident."

Another girl jumped in and started making fun of him by saying, "You look like you don't even take showers."

⏸ At this point, it'd probably be easier if I called the girls by name. But I honestly don't remember their names. They all looked like their name could be Ashley, though, so that'll do.

The first girl (Ashley A.) was getting ready to make another comment, when Karishma jumped in: "He said he was sorry, so leave him alone."

It was one of those moments when everyone stopped for a minute, and in a decent story where decent people win, there would have been a slow clap into rousing applause. But that's not what happened.

"What did you say, Gurpeet?" asked Ashley A.

"My name is Karishma," replied Karishma.

"Your name is bin Laden, terrorist," replied Ashley A.

At that moment, Karishma's eyes started tearing up. One of the other Ashleys—Ashley B.—walked over to where Karishma was sitting and looked at her food, grabbed it, and started walking around the cafeteria.

As Ashley B. walked around the cafeteria, she started

yelling, "Look! The terrorist brought her terrorist food for lunch!"

Some guy yelled, "It looks like terrorist throw-up!" The cafeteria exploded with laughter, and Karishma began crying and ran out.

I'd like to say that everyone from the safe zone decided to run around the cafeteria punching people in the face for their ignorance and racism, but we didn't. In fact, some people from the safe zone awkwardly laughed along. We didn't really blame them, though; we knew it was a form of self-defense, an attempt to avoid being the next victim.

A few of us ran after Karishma. We found her crying in the science lab down the hall. We consoled her and told her that she needed to go to the principal and also tell her parents what had happened.

A few days later, I and a few others got called to meet the principal in the auditorium. I quickly found out why we didn't meet in his office.

When we arrived, there were at least twenty people. Karishma was there with her parents, the Ashleys were there with their parents, some of our teachers were there, and a few other students who were around that day were there, including the terrorist throw-up guy.

It turns out that Karishma's family had made a complaint, to which the four girls' families had made a counter-complaint. We were asked to give our side of the story to the gathered group.

Now, some of you might be thinking this all sounds good. A public forum to address everyone's complaints—what a great way to get to the bottom of things! But keep in mind that there were some serious power dynamics at play here. Karishma, her parents, and most of us who were speaking up for her were people of color. Not only that, as you know, we were also social outcasts. Those challenging us were all white. They were also well off, popular, and connected. As much as I'd like to say these things didn't matter, the whole point of this book is that these things often matter A LOT. As they did in this case—which you'll soon see.

Ultimately, many of the people who would likely have defended Karishma ended up being too afraid to speak because of the power dynamics. Outside of me and two others, the rest of the safe-zone kids refused to speak and chose the option of going back to class to avoid potentially being attacked in the future as Karishma had been.

⏪ This was extremely disappointing, because Karishma was only in this position because she helped one of us. Until that moment, I thought we were more than outcasts. I thought we were family.

After we told our side of the story, the Ashleys and their friends gave theirs. Not only did they lie, but they painted Karishma as the villain, claiming that she threw the light saber at them.

They denied saying she was a terrorist, and as for making fun of her food, they said they had simply asked her to cover her food if she wasn't eating it, because the smell was "disturbing them."

Then the girls started crying. Their parents grabbed and hugged them and yelled at the principal for "letting them be hurt."

This was the first time I had seen the power of **white women's tears**, but it certainly wouldn't be the last.

While the families yelled at the principal, one of the teachers who often butchered Karishma's name chimed in. "I don't know Karishma to be a liar, but she certainly has been a troublemaker at times. Every morning she has a nasty attitude with me while I do my attendance. I haven't commented on it, but all of this makes sense to me now."

The principal ended up dismissing everything we said to him and told Karishma's family that they were lucky she wasn't being suspended for throwing things.

After the meeting, the teacher butchered Karishma's name every morning while she sat there and couldn't speak up for herself. The Ashleys and others made fun of her so badly that she started eating her lunch in the bathroom.

She ended up transferring to another school before the following year.

⏸ Karishma, if you're somewhere out there, reading this: I'm working on a time machine to go back and place a tack on a racist substitute teacher's seat. If you like, I can also throw your food in the face of each Ashley. Let me know.

Karishma's story always breaks my heart, because there are so many like it. Not just in terms of bullying but in terms of bullying specifically about culture and race.

Those kids didn't just think up those jokes out of nowhere; I'm sure their parents said plenty of racist things at home, and our teacher fully aligned with them because of her own cultural ignorance, not realizing she was also part of the problem.

While not every instance of problematic behavior is as intense or traumatic as what happened in the cafeteria that day—though some, sadly, are much worse—many people of color live their lives dealing with the same kinds of things in smaller doses. From being told that our names aren't normal to being told that our food is weird—it's all rooted in the idea that white cultural norms are the standard, which is not only problematic but often racist.

One of my friends spends a great deal of his time discussing topics like this one, so I thought his perspective would be good to have.

AN INTERVIEW WITH XORJE OLIVARES

*Openly gay border native, social commentator,
activist, and media personality*

One of the first things Xorje and I talked about was him
growing up as a Mexican living in America on the border.

XORJE: I love the fact that I come from the border, and I
know in depth what it's like to sit between these two cultures
of American culture and Mexican culture and have so many
things that are so outright Mexican about me.

But Xorje wasn't always knowledgeable about his own
cultural history.

XORJE: There was so much I learned about my own history
in college. Literally, here I am, a guy who grew up on the
border who should know enough about Mexican identity but
didn't even know about stuff like the Chicano movement,
certain things that are about my history. The educational
system, specifically here in the United States, told me that
it wasn't worthy of my learning. That neither I nor anybody
else in this country really needed to know about my life and
my heritage. That's been the case when we've seen these
different bills that are trying to be passed to limit either
Chicano studies or African-American studies or Asian-

American studies. There's a lot that's being done to restrict the amount of education that's being done about cultures and ethnicities that are not Eurocentric or are not specifically Anglo-American or white.

[In school] you're going to learn about white people. You're going to learn about the white history makers. You're going to learn about the white politicians. You're going to learn about everybody of note that we think needs to be told to you who happens to be white. If they're Black, if they're brown, if they're Asian, if they're Native American, [then, according to the schools] it's not as much of worth to you. I think I had a pretty American life. I think I had a pretty normal life. My parents both worked. My sister and I went to college. It seemed quite normal to me. This idea that somehow I will not achieve my full potential that this country has for me because this country is looking for something else, meaning something more white or something more straight or something more cisgender—because I don't have that, somehow I am just never going to reach it. I'm never going to get there.

What Xorje is talking about here is white standards. And not just white standards, but white heterosexual cisgender standards. If you deviate from any of these "norms," you're considered "other."

XORJE: When you think about the Fourth of July, you think of cheeseburgers. You think of hot dogs. You think of going down to the lake and having this sort of life and experience. It's, like, well, I didn't grow up eating burgers on the Fourth of July. We would have a, like, a carne asada with tortillas and tacos and guacamole and frijoles. That was what was normal for me. Let's say I were to bring anybody from outside of my hometown to see our celebration, they would think that's totally weird. I think that's the problem. This entire time, our society has made us think that we are aspiring to one certain thing.

Unlike Xorje, my Fourth of Julys were filled with grilled corn on the cob, baked macaroni and cheese, block parties, and illegal fireworks. Some of that's pretty "mainstream"—that is, white people do it, too—and some of it's specific to my culture and my upbringing. But all of it—including Xorje's carne asada and tortillas—is normal. Because "normal" is subjective. It's not the same thing for everyone, despite what white culture tries to tell us.

Many like to say America was founded on multicultural-ism—you know, the whole **melting pot** thing—but it was truly founded on whiteness and the oppression of people of color. When we begin to understand that *that* is actually our normal, it will help us raise a generation of people that won't run around a cafeteria disrespecting someone's culture because it's not their own.

I'm an American, as is Karishma, as is Xorje. Each one of us comes from a different place and a different culture and is no more or less American than the other.

Around the world, the foundation of what's "normal" typically stretches only as far as the people and cultures in front of someone, and in most places, the people and cultures in front of someone are their mirror images.

We aren't the only place that is composed of people from varied backgrounds and races. Parts of the UK are very similar in that way.

So I wanted to ask my friend Toni Adenle (Toni Tone) some of her thoughts on what's seen as normal as a person who lives in England.

AN INTERVIEW WITH TONI ADENLE (TONI TONE)

Social media content creator and public speaker

TONI: Well, one thing I can tell you is that people of color in the UK, especially young people of color, are working very hard to make sure that intellect and intelligence aren't seen as normal for just white people. With that said, though, growing up being smart wasn't something I was praised for as a Black person. One term that I actually heard commonly used as a tool or weapon against me by even other people of color was the term "coconut"—I think in America you say "Oreo"?

⏸ This totally blew my mind. I'm ready to sue Nabisco over the fact that I'm traumatized by growing up being

called an Oreo, but I can't imagine having no company to
sue because people are calling you a coconut. The UK is
rough, ha.

Toni went on to expand on what "normal" means in the
UK and how that impacts Black people there.

TONI: So, going to job interviews, for example, and people
talking about how articulate I am, and me feeling a sense of
illegitimacy from that comment, like it's not a genuine comment. I knew it wasn't a genuine comment coming from a
place of, "Oh, yeah, this was generally an articulate person,"
but almost like an element of surprise, like "I did not expect
you to be as articulate as you are based on the color of your
skin." It's not seen as normal to be anything other than what
people have seen on the news if you're Black in some spaces.

It's often as if in the UK, Blackness isn't ever supposed to
be normal. In England, what we see a lot of is microaggressions. England is very different from the United States in that
we do not often see—or I have not often seen—direct clear
racism. Now in the age of **Brexit,** people are way more vocal
about their **xenophobia** and their racism. One of the things
I've noticed young white Brits do is mock other people's culture in an attempt to make them the butt of the joke. So, for
example, someone potentially bringing in certain lunch to
school, and the first thing they do is find a way to bully them
or mock what they're eating. So, "Oh, what is that? It stinks.

It's disgusting. Why would you eat that?" It's just a round-about way of showing that something isn't normal because it isn't white.

In places like America and Britain, we have an opportunity to learn and grow by being around people who are nothing like us in many ways and very much like us in others. By having an expectation of what's normal, people build an assumption that anything else is abnormal.

We need to do away with the idea of "normal," especially when it's used as a stand-in for "mainstream" (whether that's white or anything else seen as such). Because at the heart of this difference between normal and abnormal is the belief that these so-called normal things are neutral.

An example is when white people talk about something that originates from a nonwhite culture and say, "That's Black [or Indian, or Asian, etc.]—that's not *normal*!" As if only things associated with white culture are normal—and as if white is not also a race.

◩ White people, you know that white is a race, right? And that all races are social constructs? Good—just checking.

Over the years, my favorite things about people have become the ways in which they are nothing like me.

Some of my best experiences have been when I've tried

new foods, learned to pronounce names and words that aren't familiar to me, listened to new types of music, and watched movies in languages I don't understand.

I'm asking you to protect one another and learn from one another. I'm asking you to turn "different" into the new normal, and then tell others to do the same.

5

THIS ISN'T A FAD; THIS IS MY CULTURE

Featuring Daniela Alvarez

I didn't go to parties much when I was in high school. Even though I had newfound popularity, I never trusted large group events like that. All it would take was one person getting drunk and realizing I might not be as cool as people thought I was at school for everything I had built to come crumbling down.

More important, I didn't really know how to party with the types of kids I went to school with, at least the ones who had houses big enough for parties. From what I'd heard, or maybe just seen in movies, the white kids threw the types of parties where people did keg stands, shotgunned beers, played beer pong, and listened to whatever music was popular at the time.

◀◀ For many of you, this probably sounds completely normal, but remember what you learned in the last chapter: "normal" is subjective. The few parties I went to while attending my first (predominantly nonwhite) high school were about one thing and one thing only—dancing. I don't mean organized line dancing or anything like that, I mean the type of dancing where you're way too close to your partner and if there was an adult around, they would use a ruler and a flashlight to separate the two of you.

But part of trying to keep my popularity also meant taking calculated risks so people wouldn't ask too many questions about why I never showed up to events. Which is why when I was invited to a Halloween house party my junior year, I figured I might as well go.

The party was being thrown by a student from a high school nearby. I knew some of the people who went to school there through sports and other activities.

Typically, the kids who went there came from families that were fairly wealthy. Because of that, many of them had huge homes that could accommodate a ton of people, so kids from various schools would be invited to their parties.

I didn't want to attend alone, so I asked my friend Carlos if he would come with me. I'd met Carlos during my freshman year at my prior school, and he'd become one of my closest friends.

Carlos was from a deeply proud Latinx family and lived in my neighborhood.

His dad was Puerto Rican, and his mom was Ecuadorian, and part of the reason I loved going over to his house was because the food was amazing. The other reason was because his parents loved their cultures.

We would spend hours talking about history and music from Puerto Rico and Ecuador while I stuffed my face with empanadas and other foods that made their house smell like heaven.

I loved being around his family; you could tell how much they all loved one another, especially his parents. Carlos's father worked at a factory in town and would be tired every time I saw him. But he always made sure to spend time with his children and their friends as well, and to do something sweet for his wife on a regular basis, like bringing flowers home.

Carlos was just like his parents, and honestly ahead of the curve in thinking about things such as privilege and race. Which is why I wasn't surprised by what he said when I asked him to come to the Halloween party with me.

"Hell, no. I'm not going, and you shouldn't, either."

Carlos had an issue with the white kids from the upper Westchester schools. He often complained about the fact that many of them seemed to think they were better than us. Not only that, but he said that during football games against them, some of their players would call him racial slurs on the field when referees couldn't hear.

While I knew Carlos was right about some of the kids, I felt like those weren't the ones who were throwing the party. If so, why would they invite me?

⏮ I think we've established by now that not only was I naive as hell back in high school, but I also wasn't very focused on exploring any deep and important thoughts about race. Surviving high school was my number one mission. Damn shame.

I knew I could get Carlos to change his mind, though, because, while he felt strongly about those kids, he felt more strongly about Cynthia Rodriguez, a Mexican American girl from our neighborhood who went to my school. Carlos had been in love with her for years but hadn't had the courage to speak to her.

It was simple: Get Cynthia to come with us to the party, and I would be able to talk Carlos into coming, too. Cynthia and I were on mock-trial team together and had been friends since sophomore year. It wasn't hard to talk her into going to the party, because she was happy to simply not be the only person without plans.

So I told Carlos his future wife was going, and he was in.

⏭ I mean this literally when I say "future wife." Carlos and Cynthia ended up getting married after college.

Don't believe what you hear; there are still high school
sweethearts out there.

I spent days searching for costumes with Carlos. He was
focused on impressing Cynthia, while I was focused mainly
on looking cool but not like I was trying too hard.

Carlos landed on being a fireman because he felt it would
allow him to show off his developing muscles, and I decided
to be a vampire. Not one of those cape-wearing vampires,
more like a *True Blood* vampire, where you don't know I'm a
vampire until I show you my fangs or tell you.

⏪ Basically, all I did was wear some dope sneakers,
a fly outfit, and have fangs in. Low-key, inexpensive,
and a conversation starter. I was the master of strategic
popularity.

Since Cynthia lived near us, she rode with me and Carlos
in his car the night of the party. In all of my time knowing
Carlos, I had never seen him so nervous and quiet. He didn't
say a word until we got to the house.

When we pulled up, it was like a scene out of *Animal
House* or *Old School*. It was a sea of red Solo cups and teen-
agers wearing costumes mainly made of stuff they seemed
to have found in their parents' closets. The sounds of Gwen
Stefani's song "Hollaback Girl" (ugh, this was a terrible
song) and people shouting "Go! Go! Go!" were the first

things I heard, and I immediately knew this party was everything I'd expected, sadly.

⏭ For many of you, the movies *Animal House* and *Old School* are before your time. But I'm not devoting space in the encyclopedia to them, so if you really want to know more, head to Google. As far as the song goes, I wouldn't bother searching for it. For those of you who will still inevitably search, don't forget that I warned you.

The three of us sat in the car for a second and stared at one another as if trying to decide whether we were actually going to do this instead of finding somewhere to hang out and watch bad horror movies.

Right before any of us could make a suggestion, the person who was throwing the party ran up to the car.

⏮ I think the name of the guy throwing the party was Tony, but I've met so many fratty bros like him, it's hard to remember. Let's just call him Tony.

"Fred! My man! You made it!" Tony yelled.

I stared at him blankly, annoyed and despising myself for dragging my friends to this guy's house to help me continue surviving high school and keep my popular status.

We got out of the car, and Tony led us inside to show us where to get drinks. Along the way, Tony made sure to introduce us to everyone he saw. But not in the way of "These are some people I know." More like, "Hey, look, I have friends who aren't white. I'm cool, huh?" As we met more people on our journey to the drinks, I quickly realized we were in fact the only nonwhite people there.

I would be lying if I said I expected to see many other people of color, but to be the *only* ones was both surprising and off-putting. Normally this would have been a bigger issue for Carlos, but he was more concerned with showing Cynthia he was courteous by getting her a drink. I didn't drink alcohol, so I spent my time just observing people.

I decided to give Cynthia and Carlos some alone time by walking around a bit and seeing what people were wearing and checking out the house. (I was an expert-level wingman.)

I found people dressed as the typical things: hot nurses, hot cats, hot pilots; someone was even a hot Pikachu. But what caught my eye and immediately made me pause was the sight of two white kids dressed in sombreros and traditional Mexican garments.

I walked up to them, and they greeted me by saying, "Hola," in what seemed to be their attempt at a Mexican accent. I looked at them for a second in disbelief, and then looked at what else they were wearing and carrying.

One had a belt with an empty can of beans and rice tied to it, while the other was standing next to a mop, bucket, and a sign that said WILL WORK FOR TEQUILA next to him. I still hadn't said a thing. I just stood there, dumbfounded.

> ⏸ While I wasn't the wokest kid in high school, I did know what blatant racism looked like by that point in my life. I'm just going to assume that by this point in the book, you can also see why these costumes were hugely problematic.

I eventually said, "What are you guys doing?" To which one of them replied, "What do you mean, señor?"

So I replied, "Your costumes are racist as hell."

A white girl standing with them replied, "That's not racist; it's Halloween. Besides, you're not even Mexican."

"I don't have to be Mexican for it to be racist, and I don't care if it's Halloween. Take them off," I replied.

One of them told me to make them take off the costumes, to which I was very happy to oblige, so I started walking closer, ready to fight. As I did so, Tony ran over with a few people and jumped in between me and the two guys.

> ⏸ Look, I'm a believer in nonviolence. I think most things can be resolved through conversation. But there have been times when I've been involved in physical altercations, which I'll talk more about later. This was very nearly one of those times.

Tony looked at me. "Fred, what's the problem, my dude?" (I hope you rolled your eyes at "my dude.")

I told him what was going on, and he replied by telling me it was Halloween and I was "starting trouble for no reason," because they were "just costumes."

I tried to explain to Tony that they weren't "just costumes," because they weren't costumes at all; they were racist ways of reflecting people's lives and cultures.

⏮ I'll be honest: what I likely actually said to Tony was "F*ck you! That's racist."

In the middle of my back-and-forth, Carlos and Cynthia walked over. Before I could explain what was going on, they both looked at the two guys in the Mexican costumes. Carlos immediately said, "You think that's funny?"

"You need to calm down. It's not that serious," replied one of the guys.

"It *is* that serious. You're making fun of our culture, idiot," replied Cynthia.

⏮ I'm pretty sure that was the moment Carlos knew they were meant to be.

"We are both Latino, and we are telling you it's offensive. How would you feel if someone made a costume out of you?" Cynthia continued.

One of the guys looked at me and said, "Why don't you and these spics leave?"

None of the other white people called him out for what he'd just said. They all just stood there.

⏮ It was in that moment that I knew Carlos and I were likely going to be arrested that night. Two kids of color fighting a bunch of white kids while Cynthia likely pleaded our case.

Carlos and I looked at each other, and it was as if the world froze. Without saying a word, we were playing rock, paper, scissors with our eyes to decide who was going to hit him. Before we could decide, the guy's nose was bleeding.

We looked at Cynthia, who was standing there, grabbing her hand and cursing because she had hurt herself punching the guy in the face.

⏮ I take back what I said earlier—**this** was probably the moment Carlos decided he was going to marry Cynthia.

What happened next is something of a blur, but it included Carlos and me fighting a few guys, Tony calling the police, Cynthia running to get the car, and us running out of the house, then jumping into the car and speeding off. Yeah, that about sums it up.

Lucky for us, we were gone before the police came.

⏪ I later heard the police had been receiving noise complaints and were more concerned about the party than about turning three teens of color into outlaws. (This doesn't happen often.)

On the way home, we were all silent for a while. Partially because fighting a room full of young racists is tiring work, but mainly because it was such a traumatic experience.

After a while, our silence was cut through by the sound of Cynthia crying. Carlos asked her if she was okay.

What she said next sits with me constantly, and I hope that it sits with you as well.

She replied, "All we asked them to do was respect us. Why won't they just respect us?"

Carlos didn't reply. He pulled the car over and asked me if I would drive, then got in the back seat with Cynthia while she cried on his shoulder and we drove her home.

⏸ His father taught him well.

The reason I constantly think about what Cynthia said that night is because it constantly takes place. It's not always as aggressive, disrespectful, or racist as what we dealt with that night, but it's always wrong.

This is the issue of **cultural appropriation**.

From white women wearing their hair in box braids to non–Native Americans wearing stereotypical Native American attire on Halloween (or anytime), cultural appropriation is one of the most frequently disrespectful and racist occurrences in society.

AN INTERVIEW WITH DANIELA ALVAREZ

Writer, editor, and social media manager

My friend Daniela Alvarez is one of the proudest Mexican Americans I've ever met, so I wanted to pick her brain about the issues of cultural appropriation and representation.

DANIELA: I never really saw shows or movies or any type of media piece where someone looked like me or someone looked like my dad or any member of my family or whatever. It was extremely rare. Specifically for Mexican culture, there's a lot of representation of the drug war and cartels, and that's the representation we see of my culture. Having to see those things in the media and then people playing on them with racist costumes and tropes is hard.

Following that statement, Daniela and I spoke for a while about whether there were aspects of Mexican culture she wishes people understood beyond the stereotypes.

DANIELA: I think there's a thin line between cultural exchange or appreciation and appropriation. Cinco de Mayo is a very good example. Please, I want you to patronize Mexican businesses.

I want you to buy tacos for Taco Tuesday. No one's saying you shouldn't do that. But learn about my culture and don't disrespect it in the process. You don't need to wear sombreros or dress like you're in a mariachi band to eat tacos or celebrate our Cinco de Mayo. My culture is not a costume.

While [appropriation] may not be the biggest problem we have, it definitely leads to more serious sentiments, like saying "build a wall," like being anti-immigrant and being anti-Latina, anti-Black, all these things. The dehumanization with things like appropriation has historically always led to larger issues. This is one of the reasons it's so important growing up to have friends and family of all types of ethnicities and races, because that is where you get the most perspective, from real-life relationships, real-life interactions. Respect often starts at interaction.

This lack of respect is what allowed the guys at that Halloween party to call two Latinxs "spics" while also wearing stereotypical Mexican attire, and also to claim the attire wasn't racist.

Part of what makes cultural appropriation so problematic is that it ignores the need for understanding the actual history and people who own the culture. People can learn and appreciate, but unless they are from that group, they can never fully understand.

A case study of the harm cultural appropriation causes can be found in attitudes toward **Black hair**. Historically, for instance, braids have been worn by women of African descent for hair care and for the ease they bring in hotter climates.

Because box braids haven't been a standard hairstyle for most white people, the style has often been considered unprofessional in the workforce and unacceptable in many other settings, forcing many Black women to change their hairstyles to meet these standards.

Over the years, many white women have adopted box braids as a hairstyle of choice, oftentimes making them not only acceptable in the workforce but also a staple of high fashion. Meanwhile, Black women wearing braids is still largely frowned upon (at best) or completely unacceptable (at worst), and when the style is praised on white women, Black women are often not given credit as the originators of the style.

> ⏭ Oh, remember earlier when I said that you didn't have to search for "Hollaback Girl" by Gwen Stefani? I didn't follow my own rules and went to search for the video. Guess what? There's a ton of examples of appropriation in it. So now I've changed my mind: you should go take a look and see how many instances of cultural appropriation you can spot. (I noticed at least six.)

Hair, like other aspects of culture, is part of who we are, and who we are means something. Each one of us comes from our own rich culture of food, music, and clothing, and also of triumph and struggle. Often our cultures are difficult to explain, even for the people who belong to them.

What makes a culture special is that it's not just yours; it belongs to a community of people. Your people—people who typically share an understanding of your culture and acknowledge not only the positive aspects of it but the negative, too.

Think about that the next time you're planning your Halloween costume or doing just about anything else that could end up being problematic.

■ Still not sure you know the difference between "appropriation" and "appreciation"? Here are some questions to ask yourself that might shed light on the distinction:

Who is selling the thing I want to buy? Who gets paid if I buy it?

If the money isn't going to the people whose culture is being represented, walk away.

Is the thing I want to wear used in specific ceremonies or rituals?

If so, say no!

Is the thing I want to wear or buy associated with negative cultural stereotypes?

Do your research!

Have people from within the community spoken out against white people wearing or buying the thing I want to wear or buy?

I repeat: Do your research!

If you're reading this book because you truly want to be a better white person, then consider that sometimes that might mean deciding not to do or wear or say or buy something because there's a chance doing so might hurt someone.

6

SO YOUR FRIEND IS RACIST. WHAT SHOULD YOU DO?

Featuring Jessie Daniels

By the time I started college, I was focused on having people around me who were nothing like most of the people I went to high school with. I knew that I needed a break from all of the subtle (and not so subtle) racism. So I did what made the most sense to me and tried to make as many Black friends as possible.

> ⏩ I came to find over the years that just because someone is Black or a person of color doesn't mean they actually "get it." But we will discuss this more later.

It ended up not being very hard to find Black students who were tired of racism and wanted to be around other Black people.

This was 2007, and pro-Blackness was at an all-time high in the entertainment industry, with artists such as Lupe Fiasco, Erykah Badu, Kanye West (before he was promoting white supremacy for money), and Common leading the way.

Within a few days, I had met new friends at events on campus. Of them I ended up becoming closest with two guys named Jayvon and Cory. They were from the Bronx and had gone to high school together and decided to go to the same college.

We clicked almost instantly. Where I was from was walking distance to the Bronx, so we had that in common. But everything else just seemed to work, too: we all listened to the same types of music, were interested in reading similar books, wanted to spend hours playing NBA 2K and Call of Duty, and, most important, were all focused on growing as Black people and helping our community.

I trusted them with Blackness and found myself often learning from them, because, frankly, they had been doing this longer. Jayvon's father was a Black Muslim and had been teaching him pro-Blackness since he was a child, and Cory's mom was a social worker in the Bronx who made sure he understood how white supremacist systems impact Black and brown youth.

Since we were all from the same area, we had the opportunity to hang out over the holidays back home. Which meant my two worlds could potentially collide. As I already said, I wasn't this pro-Black person in high school, so most (if not all) of my friends weren't that way. It was bad enough trying to get my family to know a more "woke" me, let alone old friends.

I'd gone from letting people call me an Oreo to protesting on campus over the disproportionate pay of Black professors. I didn't want my new friends to think I was a fraud.

Lucky for me, when I went home that first year, I didn't have to figure out what to do. All of my friends from back home were unavailable during the holidays.

⏮ I later found out they were actually available, but people had been seeing my "woke content" on Facebook and decided to steer clear. It was probably for everyone's best, anyway.

Jayvon and Cory invited me to go bowling with them and their close friend Tyler while we were home. I was excited to meet Tyler because the guys had spoken highly of him. "He just gets it," they would say.

He was also an interesting mystery for me, because I was the only one of us on Facebook at the time, so I didn't have any idea what Tyler looked like. But I naturally imagined he would be young and Black like us.

On the day we went bowling, Tyler messaged the guys to tell them that he and his girlfriend were running late, so we bowled a game without him.

As we got ready to bowl another game, Jayvon was looking behind us toward the door and yelled, "Yo, Tyler! Over here!"

I was immediately confused, because when I looked at the door, I didn't see Tyler. All I saw was a tall white guy holding hands with a short, young Black woman. The two of them started walking toward us.

"What's good, my guys! This is Denise," the tall white guy said.

"I've heard a lot about all of you," she added.

I was just standing there, flabbergasted, trying to take it all in. Not only was the close friend of my new "woke" Black friends white, but he had a Black girlfriend.

> ⏮ I can't emphasize enough how surprised I was. I'm sure my jaw literally dropped.

Tyler introduced himself to me, and I shook myself out of my surprise quickly enough to respond.

I spent the next few hours trying to understand who Tyler was and what he was about. Based on my own experiences with white people, I had a hard time understanding how a white guy was the person who had protested against racism and injustice with Jayvon and Cory in high school.

I guess Cory could feel how standoffish I was while we were bowling, because he eventually came over and spoke to me in private.

"I know what you're thinking, but he's wild cool. We wouldn't bring anyone around who isn't down for us. Get to know him," he said.

As I said, I trusted Cory and Jayvon with Blackness as a whole, and I trusted them with *my* Blackness even more. So I let my guard down and went over to Tyler and got to know him and Denise a bit more.

Jayvon and Cory were right; outside of being white, he was *just* like them—just like us. He and Denise were not only down-to-earth; they weren't afraid to address important subjects, such as their being an interracial couple.

That day we ended up hanging out for hours. Those hours became days, and eventually over the next few months, Tyler and Denise became good friends of mine.

We spent most of our time discussing politics and race, which were often brought into the conversation by Tyler. But it was never in a pandering or problematic way.

⏪ Another thing to note was that Tyler wasn't one of those white guys who think they are "down" by dressing in stereotypically Black things, like Jordans, and listening to rap. Like me, he was a huge soft-rock fan. Unlike me, he couldn't dress to save his life.

After the holidays, we hung out whenever we were all in town, and sometimes they'd visit our school, and we'd visit theirs.

That summer Tyler invited us all over to his house for a pool party.

> ◀◀ By this point, you've read a few chapters and understand my apprehension over going to a white person's home for ANYTHING.

It wasn't very difficult to decide to go. Tyler was much different from the white people I grew up with, and if anything went wrong, I had a bunch of other Black people there with me. Plus, how bad could it be if Tyler was going to be introducing Denise to his family for the first time? (They already knew she was Black.)

I decided to arrive at Tyler's house later than everyone so someone could text me if there was anything I should be aware of. (I wasn't taking any chances.)

But I never got any texts other than "where u at?"

When I got to Tyler's, I could immediately tell it was different from my other visits to white homes. Tyler greeted me at the door and said, "Took you long enough!" then shoved a burger in my hands. "Here! You're trying to get your weight up, right?"

> ◀◀ I was pretty tall and lanky at the time, so I was trying to put some weight on. Which wasn't easy as a broke college student, so I appreciated the free burger.

We walked into the house, and Tyler introduced me to a ton of his parents' friends, and eventually we walked up to his parents.

"You must be Fred! Sorry, do you prefer Frederick?" his mother said.

"Whichever you like, Ms. Matthews," I responded.

"My mother-in-law is Ms. Matthews. Just call me Marissa," she said.

Before I could wrap my mind around how pleasant this white woman was being, Tyler's father walked up, holding a plate of hot dogs and a spatula.

He was a huge man, who I knew from conversations with Tyler had played football in college. He was wearing a tank top and had tattoos all over. Upon further inspection, I could see he was wearing some sort of championship ring.

Needless to say, my racist senses were tingling. I fully expected him to ask what NBA team I played for or to say something equally racist. The new improved Black Power me was ready to fight and be kicked out of this house.

He looked at me for a second. What happened next is still one of the most surprising moments of my entire life.

"Just the guy I was waiting to see! I finished *The Audacity of Hope* last night. It was great! That Barack Obama could really make a great president!"

I was so confused, I simply replied, "Huh?"

"The book you gave Tyler about the candidate you like," he replied.

I had completely forgotten I'd given Tyler that book to read to learn more about Barack Obama. I was so dumbfounded by what was a completely new experience of white parents for me.

> ◀◀ I was a huge Barack Obama fan. I had the opportunity to get familiar with him during my freshman year and made it my life's work to get everyone to love him.

I eventually caught myself and told him I was happy he enjoyed the book. I called him "Mr. Matthews," and like his wife, he asked me to call him by his first name, Tim.

Marissa and Tim spent a great deal of time speaking to me and others that afternoon, about everything from politics to movies. For the first time, I felt like I was around a white family that respected me.

I wasn't the only one who was enjoying myself. Denise had been anxious about meeting Tyler's parents, but they hit it off. You could tell they loved her, as they were making those "you're too good for our son" jokes.

In addition to his parents' friends, some of Tyler's relatives were also there, but I hadn't paid much attention to them.

The day went on, and we were having a blast. But, as Murphy's Law says, "Whatever can go wrong will go wrong," or in the case of my life, "Whatever can go racist will go racist."

Don't steal this saying: I'm getting it trademarked. "Freddy's Law." Also, I never go by "Freddy," but you know, Murphy ... Freddy ... you get it.

At some point in the afternoon, Cory, Jayvon, and I were in the pool, and Denise was sitting on the side with her feet in the water. We had been at Tyler's house for hours with no problem, until suddenly we heard him yelling from the kitchen, where he had gone a few minutes earlier to get us some snacks.

"Don't talk about her like that!" Tyler yelled.

A woman's voice I didn't know responded, "Calm down, Tyler. It was just a question! You're going to cause a scene!"

"No, you're the one causing a scene!" Tyler replied, and then came out to the pool.

Marissa and Tim walked over, and his mother asked, "What's going on, Tyler?"

The next moment, a woman appeared from the kitchen who, Cory informed me, was Tyler's aunt.

"He's being dramatic, Marissa. I simply asked him a question," his aunt said.

"I'm not being dramatic! She's being racist toward Denise!" Tyler responded.

As soon as he said this, I started looking around for the exit. This was my cue. I was going to grab a few more of them burgers and get the hell out of there.

"I was not! I simply asked if he was serious about her," his aunt replied.

"Is that *all* you said, Mary?" Tim responded, as if he knew she was lying.

Before she could respond, Tyler said, "What you asked me was if I was serious about her. Because, you said, I couldn't marry a Black woman, especially not one as dark as her."

It was completely silent at that point. Everyone was listening, including Denise.

⏪ I knew I wouldn't have time for the exit at that point, so I figured I could hold my breath underwater until it was all over and then duck out.

Marissa looked at Denise, who was still sitting on the edge of the pool, obviously in shock and nervous.

"Did. You. Say. That. Mary?" Marissa responded.

"I mean, yes, but I—" Tyler's aunt tried to respond before Marissa cut her off by saying, "Get the hell out of my house, Mary."

She looked shocked, and immediately turned to Tyler's dad. "Tim, are you going to let her kick me out? I'm your sister."

"Yes, and I suggest you go before I put you out," Tim responded.

Tyler's aunt stood there for a moment, as if trying to get a few last whiffs of those good-ass burgers Tyler's family made.

"Now!" yelled Marissa. Tyler's aunt grabbed her things and left.

⏮ I'm a huge fan of slow claps. I try to start them all the time at the movies. If there was ever a moment for a slow clap, this was it.

The direct response to the racism of their family member was commendable, and in fact what Tyler and his parents did next was a textbook way to handle racism as a white person.

Tyler, Marissa, and Tim all went over to Denise to apologize to her and see whether she was okay. She was rightfully emotional, so Tyler took her inside and spent time with her.

Next, Tyler's parents came over to me, Cory, Jayvon, and a few other kids of color to apologize for "putting us in a traumatic situation."

◻ This was the first time white people had apologized to me for racism and done something about it. It was the last time as well. Not that I haven't dealt with racism since. (On the contrary; I've dealt with enough racism in my life to fill a book. Get it?) It's just that no other white person has taken the time to hold themselves accountable for it.

We ended up leaving the pool party shortly after that incident took place, but it wouldn't be our last time at the Matthews's home. The way they stood up against racism and defended us against their own family made us comfortable enough to continue spending time with them until they moved years later.

Being someone who supports people of color and stands against racism isn't easy. Sometimes it requires sacrifice and having difficult conversations—but that will never be as difficult as actually being *impacted* by racism.

Some people think they can be an ally while also letting the people close to them continue to be comfortable in their racism. In the case of Tyler's family, this would be like if his parents hadn't kicked his aunt out of their house but had still apologized to us for her racist behavior. That's not being an ally. That's being a coward. No one would be comfortable being racist around someone who truly stands against racism, because they would know there'd be consequences. (Like getting kicked out of their own family's home.)

Let me repeat that: *No one would be comfortable being racist around someone who truly stands against racism.* If you still have racist friends in your life, you aren't truly standing against racism.

AN INTERVIEW WITH JESSIE DANIELS

Writer and professor at the City University of New York

It's rare to find allies like the Matthews family, but there are a few. Jessie Daniels is one.

I was particularly interested in speaking to Jessie because her story is rare from all quarters. Jessie is both a white ally attempting to do her part in combating racism and the granddaughter of a member of the Ku Klux Klan.

> ⏭ I really wish I didn't have to ask you to learn more about the Klan if you aren't familiar, but we are here to grow. Which means that not all of the things you should learn about are going to be positive.

Jessie first spoke to what made her want to become the ally she is now.

JESSIE: When I was in graduate school, I worked on this project with Joe Feagin. He and a colleague of his, Mel Sikes, wrote a book called *Living with Racism*. And I was a research assistant for him and transcribed all these interviews, about two hundred or more interviews with middle-class Black Americans, describing their experiences of white racism in the contemporary setting. This was the '90s. But listening to that, to those interviews and Black interviewers with Black participants in the study—as a white woman sitting there transcribing, typing every single word of the interview, it really changed me. It was a transformative experience for me.

When I started that project, I thought racism was something that happened in the past, and when people were talking about it now, they were just making too much of it or complaining or whatever. And doing those transcripts, I realized how much of a problem it was. How damaging it was to people who were experiencing racism and discrimination, and in every story that I was typing, that I was transcribing for that work, the damage would be caused by white people.

Jessie's experience gave her a newfound perspective on what Black people in America were dealing with and who was the cause of many of our struggles. So she dedicated herself to making change. But as Jessie was working to help the people that her people were oppressing, she found out that the oppressors included people in her own family.

JESSIE: I was on a trip with my father to see a great-aunt of mine. She was the sister of my grandfather, my father's father. When I was at her house, I pulled a book off the shelf, and it was Thomas Dixon's *The Clansman*, and I said, "Aunt Marie, how come you have this book?" She's like, "Oh, I don't know. I think it was your granddad's." "Why did he have this book?" "Oh, you know, he was in that group." I was, like, "What?" It was this very kind of nonchalant revelation that my grandfather had been in the Klan.

FREDERICK JOSEPH

My father happened to be there, and I was, like, "Daddy, what's going on? He was in the Klan?" He's, like, "Yeah, they were just trying to help people." Also, very nonchalant about this revelation, and he knew that I was writing this dissertation on the Klan and hadn't told me about it, about his father. That upset me. That disturbed me. That unsettled me in a way that it didn't my family, and they were just totally casual about it. It was really for them no big deal. But I sat with that news for the next, I don't know, a couple of years or so, and just couldn't shake it, you know?

Eventually I realized that I didn't want my grandfather's last name, which was my last name, Harper, to be on the book that I was writing. So I decided to change my name. I'd never liked my first name anyway (it was Susanne), and I started looking around for white women who had fought against racism to change my name to one of theirs. And it was a short list.

I remembered someone I had read about in graduate school. Her name was Jessie Daniel Ames. She was actually from Texas, and she had started something in the early 1900s called the Association of Southern Women for the Prevention of Lynching, which was actually a white woman who was saying, "Not in our name," you know? Like, "You're lynching Black people basically in the name of protecting white women, and don't do it for me. I'm not going to stand with you; I'm not going to let you get away with this." So I decided to take Jessie Daniels as my name.

Jessie's choice may seem drastic for some, but it is inherently no different from that of the Matthews family. She identified a legacy of racism and bigotry and decided that she wasn't going to be associated with it. But more important than just walking away from it; she's doing something about it, beyond her own family.

Jessie finished up our interview by addressing why she felt it was important for her as a young white woman to make combating racism a part of her life and why it's important for other young white people to assess their privilege and power as well as the historic and current racism people have faced and continue to face.

JESSIE: I think it's so important for young white people to rethink the lessons that they've been handed down from their parents, from their elders, from their teachers, from whomever, about what it means to be white. If white people would just listen, if they would read those stories [by people of color], if they would take them in a way that they were not trying to interrupt and interject their own narrative on top of it, I think that we as white people could do less harm to other people. Right now, today, ongoing.

The world is lucky to have Jessie, as she's doing great work and is setting an example for white people around the world.

But as Jessie mentioned, she wasn't always this person,

and many white people feel exactly how Jessie once felt, that people of color, particularly Black people, are just complaining when they speak up about racism. Which is what happens when the lives of people of color are just concepts to many white people, when we are just the Black bodies they see on **the evening news,** or the Latinxs that politicians claim are illegal and taking jobs from (white) citizens.

The types of white people who accuse people of color of "complaining" are the types of white people who tell their nephew it's not okay to love and have a long-term relationship with a Black woman. They are the types of people who don't have a problem with one of their family members being a member of the KKK.

Those types of people are not me, and if you learn anything during our time together, they won't be you. Not only that, but those types of people shouldn't feel comfortable in their racism around you. Those types of people should know you're going to speak up, regardless of who they are.

Because we're the type of people who stand for something, and when it has to be, that something will be people of color.

7

NO, YOU CAN'T.
NO, YOU SHOULDN'T.
AND DON'T ASK THAT.

Featuring Joel Leon and Jemele Hill

Let me start by saying again, I'm not an advocate of violence. While I have gotten into my fair share of tussles over the years (I will never lie to y'all—they were for good reason), I prefer to talk things out. Which is why it breaks my heart every time I have to go full Dwayne "The Rock" Johnson on people.

❚❚ As I see it, there are levels to Dwayne Johnson. There's lovable him in kids' movies like *Tooth Fairy*, there's mid-level him in WWE as "The Rock," and then there's full him, shooting things, throwing things, and smacking people, which is him in the Fast and Furious series.

One of those instances happened during my freshman year of college at my school's spring concert, which I had been waiting months for. The spring concerts were the stuff of legends. Unlike at high school, where a concert meant the school band or choir performing, a concert in college meant real musical acts, famous musical acts, and, of course, after-parties.

That year, the artists Lupe Fiasco and Soulja Boy were going to be performing, which meant the party would start during the concert.

> ⏭ If you've never heard "Donk" by Soulja Boy, go listen NOW. You'll see exactly why I said the party would start during the concert.

The night of the concert, everyone on campus was excited, but none more than the freshmen. For many, this was our first-ever concert, and it was the first school "party night" for all of us. It was also the night when the campus was full of people who didn't attend our school, because students were allowed to bring guests to the show. I was attending the concert with Jayvon, Cory, and a few friends from campus.

> ⏮ So basically it was a ton of teenagers underage drinking and partying, many of whom didn't even attend the school. What could go wrong?

When we arrived at the on-campus arena, I had never seen anything like it in my life. There were thousands of people, none likely older than twenty-three, each one wearing their best outfit, and everyone seemingly looking to hook up with someone. It was everything my nineteen-year-old self had ever dreamed of.

After standing in line for about an hour, we finally made it in. It was crowded, hot, and sweaty. It was perfect.

Everyone inside was grouped with people they knew, looking around to see who they didn't know and figuring out who they wanted to know.

For the most part, we knew everyone there was to know on campus. While there were many groups, we generally all got along and had respect for one another. But because there were many people on campus and at the show that night who didn't go to our school, things felt different.

Some people used their guest passes to bring people who simply didn't fit the typical mold of the students at our school (friendly and polite), and some of the guests even seemed intent on disrespecting people that night.

Specifically, there were two white guys (not from our school) who I saw the moment I walked in; they were hanging out with this Black dude I deeply despised named Kenneth Barns.

⏮ People actually called him "KB," but this is my book, so his name is Kenneth.

Kenneth was from somewhere on Long Island and grew up in a wealthy family around a bunch of wealthy white kids, but for some reason he always tried to act tough on campus. As if he was from "the hood," where I in fact was actually from.

I hated seeing someone perpetuate the negative stereotypes of not only Black people but also where I was from, especially someone who had no reason to. But I was never more disgusted than when I saw the guys he'd brought to the show.

Kenneth and the two white guys were all wearing clothes you would only see in a parody of a rap video from 2008: baggy jeans, Jordans, gold chains, big fitted caps.

> ⏮ Mind you, at this point "urban fashion" had trended away from that style already. Which made it that much more annoying.

It was just our luck that they were right near us, and there wasn't room to get away from them. At first I was able to ignore them, as I had done with Kenneth most of the year, but then they started doing things that were impossible for me to ignore.

I was taught from a young age to respect women, part of which meant not to catcall women. It was something that my mother and grandmother made sure I understood was wrong.

If I saw someone doing it, I would typically approach them about it. But what Kenneth's friends were doing wasn't just catcalling women; they were grabbing women and being completely outrageous.

I already knew if I said something to them, it was going to be a big issue, and I didn't want to ruin the night for my friends. But after a few minutes of watching Kenneth and his white friends disrespect almost every woman walking by, I decided to approach them. I told my friends I was going to get food; just in case anything happened, I didn't want them dragged in.

As I walked up, one of the guys was talking to a class-mate of ours named Yulitza, and she looked annoyed. But I couldn't hear what they were saying over the music until I got closer.

> ⏸ Pay attention to everything that happens next, because it's a great example of just about everything white people should never do. Heck, much of it is everything *no one* should ever do.

The first thing I heard was Kenneth saying to his friend, "Her name is Yulitza. She bad, right?"

Kenneth's friend (I'm calling him Tweedledee) responded by saying, "Oh, word, Yulitza? That's mad exotic. Where you from?"

Yulitza: "I'm just Dominican. Can you leave me alone now?"

Tweedledee: "Damn, I can't just keep you company?"

Yulitza: "I'm good. My friends should be here soon."

Tweedledee: "You don't have to be all stuck up. You waiting for your man?"

Yulitza didn't respond. She started looking around as if hoping whoever she was waiting for would suddenly appear.

Kenneth's other friend (Tweedledum) finally chimed in: "She's just stuck up because she has some hair." He then proceeded to *touch* her hair.

> ◻ As I said, pay attention to things you should never do. Touching Black hair is one of them.

Yulitza yelled, "Don't touch me!"

It was at this point that I walked over and said, "You good, Yulitza?"

Before she could say anything, Kenneth got in my face. "Yeah, she's good. Why don't you relax?"

> ◄◄ No one likes being told to relax, but honestly, I'd been waiting for Kenneth to give me a reason, anyway.

I responded in the most tactful and pleasant way I could: "Get out my face before I hurt you, Kenneth." (Yes, even then I refused to call him "KB.")

Kenneth glanced at his friends as if to make sure he would be backed up in what he was going to say next. He then responded, "So what's up, then?"

I wasn't surprised that he felt bold enough to fight me in that moment. But he did seem surprised when I looked at him and his friends and said, "Who's first?"

All of them stared at me for a moment. Then Tweedledee responded, "Don't get your ass beat, my nigga."

As soon as he said it, Yulitza looked at me, and I looked at her. We both then turned toward Kenneth. Kenneth didn't seem surprised, but Yulitza and I obviously were. This white dude had just called me his *what*?

■ Now, I've already said that before college I wasn't the most woke person, and I certainly let white people slide with a lot of things. But the n-word was always off-limits for anyone who isn't Black. Doesn't matter if it's with an "a" or an "er"—
if you aren't Black, don't say it.

Also, remember, I don't condone violence, but I did what any self-respecting person would do—I went full Dwayne "The Rock" Johnson.

At some point, my friends joined in, then everyone came running over to watch. Eventually a few other people who had nothing to do with our fight started fighting.

After a few minutes (probably seconds, because brawls never last that long), one Black and two Latinx campus security guards came over with two white police officers, broke everything up, and took us outside the venue.

As soon as we got outside, the police asked Tweedledee and Tweedledum—the only white people involved—what had happened. They said that I started a brawl and was harassing them.

⏮ They both changed their voices and wording while talking to the police. They went from speaking in slang with an accent to articulating every word as if they were English professors. They knew how to play their whiteness to their favor.

The police didn't bother to ask me or my friends what happened, so I decided to speak up. "Officer, they called me a nigga," I said.

The officers looked at me for a second, and one of them said, "I suggest you stop speaking before you make this worse for yourself."

"Officer, we didn't do anything. They were grabbing women and said the n-word," I responded.

"We don't have any complaints of that," the officer responded. "All we have is a bunch of Black kids who decided they were going to jump some white kids watching a concert. Look at their faces." He pointed at the marks and bruises on Tweedledee's and Tweedledum's faces.

⏮ In all fairness, my friends and I had not only won the fight handily; we'd kicked their asses. But the officer didn't bother looking at Kenneth's face, which personally offended me, as he looked the worst, thanks to yours truly.

I began to walk closer to the officer, trying to further explain myself. "Officer, if you go and ask—"

Before I could finish, the officer had his hand on his gun holster.

"I suggest you back the f*ck up!" the officer yelled while both he and his partner gripped their gun holsters as if ready to shoot me at any second.

Before I could say anything or process the moment, Cory tapped me and whispered, "Chill. Move back."

"I'm moving back to the space I was in, and my hands are up!" I said loudly so the officers and everyone around us could hear me as I slowly stepped back.

◼ This was something that my mother taught me to do in case I was ever in a situation with a police officer like this. Something that many Black parents have taught their children during what's often known as **"the talk."** Something that doesn't always work but is an attempt to save our lives.

I stood there, shaking, trying to process what had just happened.

"Get out of here. Go home. Stay out of trouble," one of the officers said as they took their hands off their holsters.

As we walked away from the venue, we heard the officers say, "You two, get on back in there." They were speaking to Tweedledee and Tweedledum.

We also heard one of the campus security guards tell the officers that we actually attended the school and the two white guys weren't students, but the officers ignored him.

Kenneth tried to walk in with them, but the officers stopped him and said he needed to go back home. He told them he was with the two white guys, but Tweedledee and Tweedledum just looked at him and then went in.

> ⏪ It's always funny to me how that worked out for him. That's what he gets for thinking white people who say the n-word were going to defend or protect him.

As I walked away, I could only think about how unfair the moment was.

This might have been my first time fully understanding just how powerful white privilege could be and the power white people hold within the justice system.

I thought I understood. But you can never fully understand until you're in it.

I had dealt with a lot of racism in my life up to that moment, but most encounters were based in microaggressions—inherently racist or problematic things that white people had done that disrespected me but that I knew they didn't realize.

There was nothing not to realize in that moment. From touching a Black woman's hair to calling me the n-word, Tweedledee and Tweedledum's racism had been obvious. But it didn't matter.

In the eyes of the police, my friends and I (and Kenneth, too) were just a bunch of Black kids starting trouble, regardless of what had actually happened.

That night sat with me for a long time, and still does. By that point in my life, I had read countless books, watched tons of documentaries, and spent hours having important conversations about race dynamics in America, but I still wasn't prepared. You never are.

But the worst thing about what had happened was that I was *lucky*. I could have lost my life because two white guys decided to be racist asses. This is America.

There are lines that you should never cross with people from various communities, especially people of color—words you should never say, ways you should never interact.

It's a nonnegotiable understanding for many, but there are countless moments like that night at the concert, when lines aren't just crossed; they are completely ignored and disrespected. Moments when many white people simply get to do whatever they want.

AN INTERVIEW WITH JOEL LEON

Writer, author, storyteller, rapper, spoken-word artist,
and TED Talk speaker

JOEL: I didn't deal with white people until high school. And granted, the white people I dealt with were, like, in [positions of] power. Like, it was only police officers and teachers. You know? The only other white person in the world, who I never met, though, was my mom's co-worker, Miss Helen. And Miss Helen used to give my mom hand-me-downs. You know? I wouldn't even have to go school-year shopping, because I was just wearing the clothes that her older son just stopped wearing. That's all I knew of them.

This is an important point. There are many white people who live within bubbles where they don't get to interact with people of color, which we talked about earlier, but the same is sometimes true for people of color. This lack of interaction can build preconceived notions about groups of people you rarely or never deal with, from both sides. The difference is that, as Joel said, there are often power dynamics involved.

For many white people, their views of a person of color may be based on what they've seen on a show, or in a movie, or on the news, as we've discussed. But for some people of color, our first and only interactions with white people are with people in power, such as educators and law enforcement.

JOEL: I think I wasn't in the position where I really, fully understood racial dynamics until high school, when I made some white friends. Like, there are things that I'm not allowed to do because of my skin. I remember, prime example, we went to Jennifer Convertibles, just to chill.

They were sitting on the couches, and drinking soda. And I didn't do any of that. Because I was just, like, "What are they doing?" Who goes into any space and just sits on the furniture? You're not worried about staining it? I remember we left, and then we went to Central Park. And they took their shoes off, and they just started jumping in the water. And I can look back at that moment now and think about how carefree they were. And how much freedom they felt like they had. That they didn't even have to think about the consequences and repercussions of doing something that could be considered illegal, or could get them in trouble. They weren't thinking about that.

> **II** For those of you who aren't aware, Jennifer Convertibles is a furniture store. People go there to buy couches, not hang out. I really should have asked Joel why he and his friends were chilling in a Jennifer Convertibles. Anyway...

As with my story at the concert, many white people don't have to think about the repercussions of their actions in the same way that people of color do, or sometimes at all. This is the very definition of white privilege. At best, this privilege makes them feel free to do what others can't do and, at worst, to do things that disrespect or oppress others.

As was the case with Tweedledee and Tweedledum.

JOEL: Our experience with white power structures and white power dynamics and supremacy is very different [from white people's experience with those things]. Because we have to question everything before we do it; we've had to study white people forever. The reason we know them so well is because we had to. It was part of our survival. Whereas they don't have to know us or respect us.

He was right. Having the ability to survive without having to know or develop a level of respect for groups of people is part of the legacy of American racism and white privilege.

This is the same racism and white privilege that allow young white men to disrespect young Black people, yet the police are ready to kill the young Black man for standing up for himself.

This is probably part of the reason someone like Kenneth thought that he needed to let white people act a certain way around him. Because otherwise, he might not have had any friends where he was from.

Maybe Kenneth wasn't much different from me during my Carlton phase. We may have both been survivors trying to get by, and that meant lessening ourselves for the white people around us. Two people, damaged by the same system.

> ⏪ Though I wouldn't have ever gone to the depths that Kenneth went.

Those young white men didn't have to understand or respect him, but there is a value for those who decide to, which is something Joel gave his thoughts on.

JOEL: For me, I think I've benefited from having a diverse circle or grouping of friends and people that I learn from. It enhances my global experience. And it enhances my local experience. There's so much to be benefited from being more inclusive. You'll grow more. You'll just be a better human being. You'll be a better parent. You'll be a better partner.

If I'm being honest with you, white people don't *have* to change; they will be fine without doing so. But white people *should* change, because just being *fine* shouldn't be good enough.

Which is something I discussed with journalist Jemele Hill.

AN INTERVIEW WITH JEMELE HILL

Journalist, host, sports expert, and overall dope person

JEMELE: Learning about other people allows us to have more empathy for the other person, and therefore more growth, in that as you become more empathetic, I think, you become more fully human and fully whole because you start to understand how the world works. And I thought that was the mission, why we got all put here together: to understand how this world works. Being homogenous doesn't teach you that. If we all went through different experiences all the time, and we were all getting exactly alike, how would we ever grow? We wouldn't.

Most people don't look at the world the way Jemele and Joel do. So I asked her why she feels so many people would rather not see color than learn about others.

JEMELE: I think part of the reason why people say that they don't see color, or they don't want to see race, or they never even want to be challenged outside of that viewpoint, is because not only does it require you to do some extra thinking—some critical thinking, to have empathy that you didn't want to have, maybe toward not just the people that you know but maybe in some cases the people that you don't know—it also makes a demand of you, and people aren't good with that. Maybe especially demand where at some point you have to kind of look at yourself a little bit and understand how the way you have viewed things may have contributed to the poor way in which we treat race in this country.

I agree with Jemele—fear and not wanting to take accountability are large reasons people don't want to grow in terms of race.

Jemele gave me a final thought on why young white people should take the opportunity to learn about other races and grow in ways many of their predecessors haven't.

JEMELE: I guess I would say to young people especially, they have an opportunity for growth that they should always welcome. They should want to learn these things. And once they learn how everybody's experiences are interconnected—and I guess it's kind of the differences that I don't think they see the beauty in. Again, we are definitely all different, and that's fine, and that's okay, but those differences are actually quite interconnected, and maybe if they understood that part of it, they wouldn't always think of learning about race or talking about race as something that was automatically supposed to be divisive. Quite the opposite; it's actually supposed to bring us all together, despite the crowd constantly bellowing that the real racists are the people who talk about race.

There is a world that we can create that is stronger and more enjoyable if we all learn from one another and develop understanding that doesn't allow us to simply survive but to thrive.

A world where maybe I learned Tweedledee's and Tweedledum's actual names, because it's obvious we were into similar music, since we were all at the same concert.

A world where two young white men know they shouldn't touch a Black woman's hair or call a Black man the n-word.

A world where that night is something we all remember for the right reasons. Maybe in that world, we all became friends that night.

That's not this world, but if we understand what we can't do to one another and how to treat each other better, it can be. If you're still reading, I'm sure that's because you think so, too.

8

NO, I DIDN'T GET HERE
BY AFFIRMATIVE ACTION
(AND IF I DID, SO WHAT?)

Featuring Jamira Burley

There's a YouTube video I watched for the first time in early high school that changed my perception of almost everything I knew. The video was of a college lecture about racism and white privilege in America.

⏮ This was back when YouTube started, so I'd find all sorts of random things to watch. I'd love to share a link to that video, but it seems to have disappeared from YouTube in the intervening years, though videos about similar experiments exist. And, yes, I'm that old that I remember when YouTube started.

In the video, a professor gathered his class and put a garbage can in the middle of the room. He then asked each student to take a piece of paper and crumple it into a ball. After that, he asked the students to take the ball and throw it into the trash from any distance they would like. Students did as instructed and shot from various places in the room.

⏮ Obviously, many people shot from far random places and shouted, "Kobe!" Because that's what ballers do.

Next, he asked the students to crumple another piece of paper, but this time he told them he would randomly choose someone who makes the shot to have a day off from class the following week. Each of the students shot from much closer this time; some even dunked the paper in.

Then he told the class that whoever made the next shot would get an A added to their semester grades. He also told them that they would have three opportunities to make a shot.

They thought he was joking (so did I), until he promised them he wasn't and they could tell the dean if no one got the promised bonus grade.

Each student crumpled up three pieces of paper and got as close as they possibly could to ensure they wouldn't miss.

But before anyone could take a shot, the professor started to point at students and ask what their race was. All of the students who identified as white were placed in random spots around the lecture hall, some so far from the trash can that it was almost impossible for them to make the shot.

But each student who didn't identify as white was allowed to stay where they were.

He then decided that only some of the white students he moved would have an opportunity to take more than one shot. He walked around the room and randomly took one crumpled paper ball from some students and two from others.

As he did this, the white students started to complain. In response to their complaints, he forced some of them to cover their eyes for their shot.

He then randomly chose students of color who were close to someone near the garbage can and told them that if the person next to them made it, they didn't have to shoot and they would also receive the A. But in the unlikely event that the person missed, he would still allow them both to take their full number of shots.

When he told the students to shoot, only two of the white students made it, while every student of color made the shot.

The white students were in an uproar. Some were cursing, others were saying they weren't coming back to the class, and one student said he was going to complain about the class to the school administration.

The professor told the students he'd already spoken

to the administration, and they had no problem with the lesson.

He then asked everyone to sit down and to congratulate the students who would receive the A. He asked the white students how they felt, and many responded with words like "unfair," "angry," and "cheated."

He then asked the students of color to raise their hand if they had a thought on what the experience felt like to them. The very first person to respond said, "America." He asked her to explain, and she said, "It feels like how America treats us versus them."

As she said that, I found myself nodding along with the students of color who were in the video.

The professor responded, "This was a demonstration of the impact of systemic racism and white privilege. Most of you just experienced a fraction of what Black and brown people in America face every day in our justice system, education system, and professional system. In fact, that fraction was so difficult for you that you forgot that you were in a lesson about racism. White people have oppressed their way into a head start from slavery to **mass incarceration**. Y'all are lucky you even got to take a shot; most Black people don't even get that."

> ❚❚ I really wish that professor was my uncle or something. If you're out there, Professor, you're the man, brother!

I spent that entire night thinking about how powerful that lesson was. It gave clarity to so much in my own life. I went to school and tried to get people to watch the video. No one was interested.

> ⏸ If you're someone reading this book whom I begged to watch the video, I ended up getting you anyway, because it would have been easier watching it than reading about it.

While most people I knew never saw the video, it changed me forever. I had never really understood how to articulate my feelings about how I was impacted by the world around me. It's not that I didn't know about racism, the power of white people, or some of the lasting effects of slavery. Those things were common sense to me.

But the YouTube video was a drilled-down demonstration of why my mother and grandmother had always told me, "Black people have to work two times harder and be twice as good."

They made sure it wasn't just a phrase; it was a way of life. They would make sure that I was talented and skilled enough in school to the point where the system designed against the success of Black and brown people would still be forced to give me an opportunity.

When I was growing up, they made me read everything, watch every documentary, and if I seemed to have a talent or passion for something, they would find a way to make sure I got the opportunity to try it. I played instruments, I sang in the choir, I was in the drama club, I was in a poetry class, I did it all, and I did it well.

But there was nothing I was better at than debating and problem solving. Everyone told my mother I had a natural gift for arguing points (I'm not sure how much of a compliment that was) and that we should think about my becoming a lawyer. So that's what we did.

When I was around twelve years old, I started reading everything I could to help me become a great lawyer. I wanted to help provide a better life for my family, and that was going to be the way. Everything I read told me great lawyers had to also be great writers (this was a lie) and be well versed in not only law but history as well.

I started practicing my writing every day and reading history books and court documents from old highly public cases. I was also watching reality TV court shows and dramas like *The Practice*, which didn't teach me very much but sure did make me want to be a famous lawyer.

> ⏭ I can't stress enough how amazing a day filled with watching *Judge Mathis* and *Judge Judy* can be. Thank me later.

I read countless cases, but none interested me more than civil rights cases, and no lawyer captured my attention like Thurgood Marshall.

> ⬤ I'm hoping you actually google something every time I ask you to, seeing as I have impeccable taste. But I can't take a chance on you not learning more about Thurgood, so I'm giving you his background here.
>
> Thurgood Marshall was the first African-American Supreme Court justice. He played a vital part in ending legal segregation during the civil rights movement through the landmark 1954 case *Brown v. Board of Education* and founded the NAACP (National Association for the Advancement of Colored People) Legal Defense and Education Fund.
>
> You're welcome.

I loved everything about Thurgood. He was brilliant and stylish, and he didn't take crap from anyone—not even white people during segregation. I wanted to be just like him, so I kept working.

By the time I got to high school, I had read every constitutional law book available in the school district and many that weren't. I even taught myself to write mock-case briefs. Needless to say, I was destined to try out for the mock-trial team (the debate team) in high school.

⏮ If you feel bad because it sounds like I didn't have friends, don't worry: I had tons of friends—finally.

Over the years as I "glowed up," by growing into my face and sprouting to six feet my freshman year, I realized being nerdy was still my jam. So I ran with it, and now I was far more confident in my nerdiness because of my appearance.

Our mock-trial team was interesting, because while the school was largely white, the team wasn't. As I remember it, there may have been only one white person on the team. All of the rest of us were kids of color. Regardless of what the team's makeup was, we were damn good, and I was our best. (Cocky, but true.)

During my time on the team, we demolished schools in our district. It wasn't even close. We were so good that during my junior year, we made the county tournament, which was held in upper Westchester at one of their high schools that looked like a college campus. (I've told y'all they have money.)

There were eight other schools at the event. We were the only school from lower Westchester that made the tournament. In fact, we were the first school from lower Westchester that had ever made it.

⏸ We were the descendants of Yonkers's wildest dreams, ha. I'm sure this joke will go over many heads. But when you get it, you'll come back and go, "Ooooh."

Leading up to the tournament, I knew we were going to win. I felt like there was literally nothing that could stop us.

Then imposter syndrome set in.

I remember walking into the school and feeling like we were all extremely out of place. Not only did we have the only nonwhite team; we also were underdressed.

We had been wearing casual clothes, like jeans and sneakers, to every match for more than a year against schools in our district, so we wore the same to the tournament. But everyone else was wearing business attire and full-on suits.

⏪ I don't mean oversize suits that they pulled out of their parents' closets, like Donald Trump wears. These kids had custom-tailored pieces for this event. It looked like they were all going to interview for a job at a top law firm.

All of the other students were staring at us. I could see that my team was feeling it, too.

Our first match, about an hour after we arrived, was against the school that had won the tournament the year before. We got to the room, and our opponents were already there.

A few parents were with their children's teams, and some were standing near us. A few of us overheard two of the parents talking to one of the students on the other team before we got started, and what we heard devastated us.

The student told the two parents that she was nervous about the first match. One of the parents looked over at us and said, "Don't worry, they're probably just the **affirmative action** kids. They have to do that sometimes. They have to say they're giving a chance to minorities, so they stick them in, even if they aren't as good."

One of my teammates started crying and went to the bathroom after overhearing this.

I'm pretty sure those parents knew we could hear and did that to throw us off our game, or maybe they didn't. Either way, it was a trash way to treat a bunch of kids.

Our coach asked why my teammate was crying, and we told him what we'd overheard. He had someone go get her out of the bathroom and gave us a talk.

He told us that we were just as good as, if not better than, the other team, and neither they nor he could understand as white people how hard it is to be nonwhite and try to do something while held back by racism.

He then explained that even when programs like affirmative action did help people like us, it was because we deserved it, not because it was some sort of handout.

◼ I believe, based on America's history, there's no such thing as a handout to people of color, especially Black and Native American people. But that's a whole different book topic. *Cough*, reparations.

After his talk, I looked at my coach and said, "It sounds like you watched the YouTube video, too!"

"What video?" he responded.

"Never mind," I said.

⏸ Sigh—no one saw that video! If any of you find it, please feel free to send me the link.

After our coach's talk, we were ready. This wasn't just about winning a mock-trial match; this was about kicking racism in the mouth. This was our Thurgood Marshall moment, our *Brown v. Board of Education*!

⏸ Okay, maybe not, but you get the point.

We ended up tearing that school apart in the first match, and then we tore the next school apart, and then we made the last school look foolish in the final round. We didn't have the tutors, the new textbooks, or the technology of our white opponents; we were just *better*. We had worked harder and were more talented than the other teams, and it showed.

While winning the tournament was nice, nothing was better than seeing the looks on the faces of the people who had been looking down on us since we walked in. As if we were lucky to be in their presence.

I took that day with me, and I still hold it close. It's

important to me because, while it wasn't the first time I was underestimated because of my race, it was the first time anyone had said I was handed anything because of it.

This has since been a pattern in my life as people have tried to write off my success and the success of other people of color as the result of a handout. But programs like affirmative action, which were put in place to right historical wrongs, are not *handouts*. Think back to that YouTube video. Affirmative action isn't putting all the Black kids' balls in the basket for them. It's not even moving all the Black kids to the front row. Affirmative action is letting *some* Black kids sit in the same row as *most* of the white kids. It's giving an opportunity to a person who would not otherwise have it because of discriminatory systems. Programs like affirmative action are actually just a small way to right historical wrongs.

AN INTERVIEW WITH JAMIRA BURLEY

Activist and social impact consultant

I spoke with activist Jamira Burley about her thoughts on affirmative action, and why it's important that people of color be given opportunities in traditionally white spaces.

JAMIRA: At every institutional level, there are opportunities that are supposed to address those who are the most marginalized, those who are the most in need of actually getting access to those resources. So whether you're talking about welfare or whether you're talking about transportation, you're talking about legal representation. What we see oftentimes is that there are gates—I should say there are barriers to entry.

For instance, if a young person wants to get access to opportunities for school, they have to have money for transportation and/or they have to meet with someone to fill out paperwork. That normally requires them to have access to their birth certificate, which normally they don't. Also what we've often seen is that those resources are actually being taken up by others, many times by middle-class white folks, especially women, because white women are actually beneficiaries of affirmative action. We don't talk about that enough.

The point that Jamira made about who affirmative action also—and at times more so—serves is important. There is a narrative that affirmative action and programs like it, such as welfare, were created to help Black people. But in reality many of these programs benefit white women and poor whites more than other groups.

There are more white women and poor white people in America than there are Black or brown people combined, so these programs serve a great number of white people. Yet many white people who oppose the programs or use them as an example of a handout act as if only people of color are benefiting.

▶▶ These types of false narratives are discussed in the encyclopedia.

As I mentioned earlier, there is often the misconception that if someone is benefiting from programs like affirmative action, they are getting an opportunity that they don't deserve. Which is the furthest thing from true.

JAMIRA: Affirmative action is actually giving a gateway for institutions to be much more intentional when looking at the scope with which they've done their recruitment, their hiring, and actually say, "We need to take a closer look at why our internal biases have allowed us to look past minority candidates." And so it was not to say that these minority candidates don't have the qualifications. Oftentimes they're actually more qualified than their supervisors. Right? We see that with how Black men who could have a college degree are less likely to get a job versus white men who have a prison record or simply a high school diploma.

So for me, affirmative action isn't a negative thing. I think we've allowed the far right, our opposition typically, to create this narrative that those who get access to affirmative action are unequipped to have those jobs and are only there because of their racial, sexual, or gender identity, which is bullsh*t, because oftentimes when I'm the only one, I'm there for a reason, because those who are there can't do the job that I've been hired to do.

One of the aspects of programs like affirmative action that gets overlooked is the positive impact they have, not only on communities of color but on the white spaces that they are bringing diversity to. As we've discussed, individuals are stronger and better for having more people around them who aren't just like them. But so are places such as schools and businesses.

JAMIRA: When we think about culture, who drives the culture? Who creates the culture? It is people of color. And so the reason why it's an important thing for organizations, nonprofits, companies, or entertainers or whatever to engage folks of color is because we can culturally bring something to that organization, that environment, that they have been lacking, which actually creates creativity, it drives innovation, and it actually improves the conditions for all of us and not just for the chosen few.

America is no different from the classroom in that YouTube video. It's a high-stakes game of seeing who can shoot the paper into the basket, who has to work harder to make the shot, and who gets to shoot at all.

But the basket isn't always an A in a class or a home in a wealthy area or a job. Things like who gets a chance to attend college or who gets called for an interview can end up having a huge impact on a person's quality of life. And for some, the consequences can even be a matter of life and death.

The idea that affirmative action is a negative thing, while some people have not had to work at all for their success, is based in racism. As is the idea that these programs serve people of color primarily.

Programs like affirmative action are a small step toward course-correcting hundreds of years of oppression by people who not only get to take all the shots but also get to choose where they place the garbage can.

For so many little Black and brown boys and girls, "working twice as hard and being twice as good" isn't enough. We also need programs to make sure our voices get to be heard.

We live in a country founded on land stolen from Native Americans and built by people stolen from Africa. A country that claims the value of "liberty and justice for all."

But until "all" stops being "some," the least America can do is have programs in place to give people a chance to make a shot.

9

LET'S NOT DO OPPRESSION OLYMPICS

Featuring Saira Rao

By the time I got to college, I was still planning on becoming a lawyer, which meant taking on a major that would help me get there. When I started my freshman year, I learned that some students were actually taking on two majors, so of course my competitive juices started flowing, and I did the same.

I majored in political science and creative writing, which made sense for someone on a trajectory to be the next overpaid celebrity lawyer who would one day have his own show about a high-powered attorney living in New York City.

⏮ I'm not sure what I would have called the show, but the intro would have had a real gritty '90s New York City vibe with a theme song by Mobb Deep. (If you don't know who Mobb Deep is, this is another way that society has failed you. But don't worry: I've included a must-listen playlist in the back of the book. Thank me later.)

Another thing I decided was to continue doing as many extracurriculars as possible, not just because I was still an overzealous teen but also because some extracurriculars paid stipends, and I was a very, *very* broke student.

There was only one issue: most of the opportunities for stipends were given to athletes, student government members, or members of dorm government. (Yes, our housing had governments.) Although I was in my athletic prime, there wasn't much of a shot of walking on to any sports teams at a D1 school. But school and dorm politics I was made for, as I had done politics throughout high school.

Like any other level of politics, college campus politics is a popularity game. It's all about who you know and who will tell other people to vote for you. I was lucky enough to be a part of a group of friends that very quickly became popular on campus. There was also my understanding of how to use Facebook and other digital tools to get people to know and like me (or at least just be familiar with my name).

⏮ Facebook had just started having wide appeal the summer before my freshman year, so not many people knew how to use it for evil yet. But I did. *Evil laugh*

Come to think of it, I might have built the roadmap for propaganda in the 2016 election. Oh, God... Am I responsible for Donald Trump?!

Because I had studied graphic design in high school, I was able to make logos, banners, and other campaign materials that my friends and I posted on Facebook, placed around the campus, and handed out at events.

My competition stood no chance; I handily won my race to join the student government and solidified my place as a stipend-earning student. I was a made man.

The race for dorm government was a few weeks later, and it proved to be far more difficult.

Our campus had five dorms, which students were divided into based on their major, extracurricular activities, and a survey we'd filled out while applying for housing.

Most of the students in the dorms were freshmen or sophomores, as juniors and seniors generally lived off campus. It was a way to keep people who would likely have similar personalities together and make building bonds and transitioning into college easier.

I'm not going to say this wasn't a good tactic by the school. In theory it should work. They did enough to try to place people in situations to forge life-long friendships, I suppose.

But honestly, at eighteen, the last thing most of us wanted to do was talk about life goals and career trajectories.

Making friends was about who had extra Xbox controllers or, for some, fake IDs for beer.

> ◘ Hi, Reader,
> Don't underage drink. Especially if it's Natty Ice or Everclear; you'll thank me one day.
> Love,
> Fred

I was placed in a dorm with other political science and double majors, as well as with business majors, pre-law students, pre-med students, and all the other kids whose families had probably told them what their careers were going to be since they were able to walk.

That said, there was one way that almost all of the people living in my dorm were similar: everyone was super ambitious, super broke, and determined to find ways to get stipends.

> ▮▮ You'll find being broke in college is a common theme, because the stuff is too expensive for anyone not from a wealthy family. Even if you get a full ride, keeping yourself alive is expensive. Say it with me:
> FREE COLLEGE FOR ALL.

One thing I did have going for me was that the administration at my school and more particularly my dorm was going through what much of the rest of the country was going through. Something I like to call the Obama Effect.

This was 2007, and while Barack Obama wasn't president yet, many people loved him and were excited about the possibility of him as president. He was attractive, smart, well spoken, had graduated from top schools, and was half Black. The last part is important, because it helped create some type of awakening for many white people.

For some white people, it seemed like it was the first time they had ever realized that people who weren't white just might be worthy of respect and given access for their talent (sigh).

> ⏸ One thing I hated about this era was the number of times people would call me a "young Barack Obama." While I'm sure they thought it was a compliment, to me it was just them saying I was similar to the only person who looks like me that they ever thought was intelligent.

The Obama Effect made people at my school want to find their own young Obamas who could help score them some diversity points. While it was deeply problematic, it was also an opportunity.

The residence directors and resident assistants of my dorm put up signs and let people know that they wanted our dorm government to represent "people from all backgrounds." Which was a very politically correct way of saying, "The students who have run our dorm have always been white, and we need something else."

So when I decided to run for president of the dorm, many people in the administration figured they were going to get their Obama. While they couldn't openly say they were rooting for me, the administration did make sure I had the tools to succeed, and then some.

> ⏮ This may sound like there was some type of election influencing going on, but it was really just RAs telling me where I could get extra materials, letting me print flyers for free, and things like that.

There were four people running against me for the position, two of whom weren't putting forth any effort to win; they were just hoping that people would randomly vote for them. The other two were not only putting forth effort; they were obsessed with winning. Their names were Abbie and Parker.

Abbie was a young white woman from California, and Parker was a young white openly gay guy from Maine. Both of them were also studying political science.

While the rest of us wanted the position in order to help pay for school and survive, neither of them needed it for that. They wanted the position because it was a way of adding to their résumés. And in Abbie's case, she had an older sister who had been president of the dorm some years earlier, and she wanted to keep the legacy going.

The two of them came from well-off families, and it showed. They weren't only printing flyers and using Facebook; they had purchased things like cookies and pens with their names on them, as if they were running for mayor.

> ◄◄ Which is part of the reason the residence staff was giving me some help, because otherwise I wouldn't have been in the race. How do you compete with free cookies and pens?

The other issue the residence staff had was that neither Abbie nor Parker wanted to do anything to help the residents of color, and most of the staff were people of color who were former residents. I was basically the people's champion.

> ◄◄ That was actually what my campaign slogan for both student government and dorm government was: Frederick Joseph, "The People's Champion."

At some point during campaigning, Abbie and Parker found out that I was being helped by the residence staff, and they made a complaint to the administration together.

The administration called a meeting to decide not only whether I should be disqualified from running for the position but also whether there should be repercussions for the residence staff members who had given me help.

⏪ Yes, all of this because they were trying to help my broke ass print flyers and design signs.

The meeting included Abbie, Parker, me, the residence staff, the director of residence life, and two of the school deans. It was, to say the least, A LOT.

The meeting was set up in the style of a debate, to a certain extent, with the deans and the director of residence life basically acting as judges.

Abbie and Parker went first and made the point that they felt I was being helped because I'm Black, and the residence staff wanted them to lose because they're white, and that was reverse racism.

⏩ "Reverse racism" is not actually a thing. But we will talk more about that in a bit.

While the entire moment was annoying, there couldn't have been a better situation for me to be in. Not only was I a debate master, but by that time, I had also spent most of my free time studying and learning about race. I was ready to rip them apart. Little did I know, so was the residence life staff.

Before I went up to speak, the residence life team had

the opportunity to make their case. They explained that there were no policies against helping provide resources for students. They also explained that helping to even the playing field in this case was in the best interests of the students in the building who were from minority groups, as I was the candidate most likely to care about and plan to help them.

They also mentioned the fact that the dorm had never had a person of color as president, but it had the largest number of students of color of all the dorms.

The idea that I was the only candidate who could understand the residents from minority groups didn't sit well with Abbie and Parker. Both of them jumped up to speak to the fact that Abbie was female and Parker was gay. They then went on to say that maybe I didn't get it because I was a "straight guy."

Once they finished, I had an opportunity to speak.

⏭️ You've probably seen people get dunked on before, whether in real life or on video. It's embarrassing for the person getting dunked on, and one of the greatest moments ever for the person doing the dunking. It shows that one person has dominance in one moment, in front of everyone around.

That pales in comparison to what I did to Abbie and Parker that day. I obliterated them and left what was remaining as a testament to everyone around me that I am not to be messed with.

For a visual demonstration that comes close to what I did, go search for Shawn Kemp dunking on Alton Lister. It's the only thing close. Don't even read on until you do it.

Okay, I'm going to trust that you've done it, so let's continue. Enter Frederick Joseph, attorney-at-law.

I started by addressing the fact that they used the idea of reverse racism. I explained that reverse racism doesn't exist; if something is racist, it is just racist. To argue that something is an example of *reverse* racism would mean that the person with the issue knows that "normal" racism—aka *racism*—doesn't affect them.

And the truth is, racism and racist systems in America *don't* adversely impact white people. This is because all aspects of racism in America are rooted in white supremacy and are designed to negatively impact everyone *except* white people.

Abbie jumped up and said that this was "like affirmative action, which is reverse racism."

I shot this down, too. I explained that affirmative action and programs like it were not reverse racism—which, again, *isn't actually a thing*; they were created to correct the unbalance caused by racism and white supremacy. Then I explained that the term "reverse racism" actually became popular during the time that affirmative action was created because of a backlash by white people who were mad that programs were created to help people of color prosper.

I then went on to educate them about the fact that those programs don't help only people of color—they also help other minority groups, such as women and people who are gay. So much for reverse racism.

At this point, Abbie smartly backed off the argument that what was happening was racist and instead argued that she and Parker *also* should have gotten help, then, since she was a woman and Parker was gay.

I actually agreed with her on this point and told her as much—but before she could get too excited, I pointed out that that was an argument for each candidate having a fair chance and equal resources. Which meant not giving out cookies and pens while others are drawing posters.

Oh, but I wasn't done yet, my friends! I also added that thinking things like reverse racism existed actually demonstrated how ill qualified they both were to represent students of color.

⏮ Frederick drives the lane and dunks on two defenders! The crowd goes wild!

After the meeting, the administrators decided that the election in our dorm and all dorms on campus should be fair. This meant that candidates couldn't receive disproportionate resources from staff; each had to be equally resourced with printing and the other things I was receiving. But "fair" also meant that candidates couldn't campaign beyond the parameters set, which included no personally financed gifts, such as cookies and pens.

Abbie and Parker were pissed; their plan had backfired. Not only were they not able to use the one advantage they had over me (money), but I also let students know that my opponents had tried to stop our dorm from having its first president of color because they felt like the help I was given was reverse racism.

Not only did the residents of color get angry at them, but so did the white students who couldn't believe that Abbie and Parker had tried to stop "our school's own Barack Obama."

⏪ This was the only time I didn't mind the Barack Obama stereotype. Shout-out to the Obama Effect!

Some students even created a Facebook page called "You're Still White," which was filled with people discussing times that white people said they understood the problems of people of color because they were women or gay.

I ended up winning the election in a landslide, with 70 percent of the vote, and so did all other candidates of color who were running for dorm positions on campus.

Abbie's and Parker's inability to understand their privilege helped spark a political revolution on campus. But potentially more important, it helped kick-start much-needed conversations about race and the **intersections** of race, gender, and sexual orientation.

AN INTERVIEW WITH SAIRA RAO

Author and entrepreneur

There are only a few people whom I personally admire when it comes to conversations about these intersections and privilege, and one of them is Saira Rao.

SAIRA: White men, without a doubt, are the most powerful group in America. But white women enjoy as much white privilege as white men. White men are rightfully always on the hook. White women wouldn't argue that white men aren't racist, right? We just all assume that white men are racist. But white women have been let off the hook for that entire thing all this time until recently. Susan B. Anthony was one of the most racist people on the planet. And she is a white feminist icon; she's a god, right?

There were a few times while writing this book that I had to stand back in awe of something that was said to me in an interview, and Saira's first two sentences were one of those times. In just a few words, she was able to capture the essence of how white people who aren't straight men exist within and benefit from white supremacy.

SAIRA: White women have not only been let off scot-free, they are heralded for their innate goodness. For being NICE.

Saira next shared her thoughts on how privilege and power work in situations where you have white minorities (like women or members of the LGBTQ community) who believe they are more oppressed than someone who is Black or another racial minority.

SAIRA: We just erase history and create new stuff, and then everyone pretends like that's the reality. It's white women who get Black men killed all the time. Let's not forget Emmett Till. It's white women who are picking up the phone and calling 911 on Black people sitting and standing and breathing and having coffee at Starbucks. If you are a white woman, you are on the receiving end of oppression, being a woman, but can be on the giving end of oppression because you are white. As an Asian woman, I am on the receiving end of oppression, being brown and being a woman, but can be on the giving end of anti-Black racism.

It's not complicated.

Saira then shared a story that speaks to how powerful white supremacy and racism are and the generational impact of oppression.

SAIRA: When I was nine, a white boy in my class asked me to go out with him, and I said yes. And the next day, he came to school and asked me to meet him in the library, and I was, like, "Oh my God, so psyched, he's brought me Skittles or something." And I met him in the library, and he told me he couldn't go with me anymore because his mom said he couldn't go with a Black girl. [*Sidenote: Saira is Indian, not Black.*] And so I literally remember thinking to myself, *His mom is right; she's doing what's best for him,* as if telling him, "Eat your vegetables and get some exercise; don't associate yourself with Saira." And I got home—and I didn't cry all day—but I sat on my front stoop, weeping, and I took a rock and started rubbing my arm, trying to rub the brown off of my skin. And my mom came home from work in her sari—and she was called all sorts of things by people there, who then she had to give rectal exams to.

So I just think about the humiliation she had to live through. And she said on her death bed to me six, seven, years ago, one of the worst memories of her life was arriving home that day and seeing me on the stairs, bleeding, saying to her—and I said to her—"This is your fault." And I pointed at my skin, and I was like, "This is your fault." And you know what she said to me? "You're right." And that was the end. She didn't try to tell me to love myself or that guy was wrong, because she had self-loathing, because she was internally oppressed. You'll recall the British colonialism of India. Okay? So, that's in the '80s in Richmond, Virginia.

In 2016, in Denver, in super-liberal Denver, Colorado, I come down the stairs, and my son, who at the time was seven, six or seven, is standing in my kitchen, and he has unleashed two tubes of sunscreen all over his body, rubbed it all over his body. And I was, like, "What are you doing?" And he goes,

"Mom, look, I'm finally white." And I was, like, "Oh my God, nothing has changed. Nothing has changed."

Saira's points and quotes help frame not only the impact of generations of trauma from white supremacy but also why it's crucial that we understand the intersections of privilege and power among white people.

It's a difficult conversation, and one that people like Abbie and Parker are often not prepared to have. It's a conversation that forces white people to reflect on identity, which is something that isn't easy for anyone.

As a cis heterosexual Black man, I have to assess the privilege and power I have compared with women and people in the LGBTQ community, while also assessing the other aspects of their identity. Because, while I face more oppression than Abbie because she's a white woman, I face less oppression than Black women. The same way Abbie faces more oppression than Parker because he is a white man, still a part of the group that ultimately has a great deal of power. Only a straight white man would deal with less oppression, because that group holds the most power.

And Abbie, Parker, and I each face far less discrimination than Black transgender women, who have to deal with the oppression of white supremacy, transphobia, and the patriarchy.

In one way or another, we all have some type of privilege or power in relation to someone else, but most of us aren't reflecting on that. Most of us aren't thinking about how we may be hurting someone else, how we may be ignoring someone else, how we may be oppressing someone else.

It's a difficult conversation because it requires us not only to treat others better but to hold ourselves accountable.

It's hard to see the role we play in someone else's struggle while we are busy fighting for ourselves or our people.

But we have to learn to see with new eyes, hear with new ears, and find new ways to trust other people's words when they tell us and show us how we're hurting them. Because doing the right thing sometimes means putting the pain of others before our own, especially if we are part of creating it.

10

WE DON'T CARE WHAT YOUR BLACK, BROWN, OR ASIAN FRIEND SAID WAS OKAY (F.U.B.U.)

Featuring Tarell Alvin McCraney

I love music. I know a lot of people say that, but I really love music, and I have ever since I was a child.

My earliest memories are of me feeling the vibrations of the music that people would play around me. I can still remember being a child and understanding the energy in the room based on what people were listening to. Their joy, their pain, or their loneliness.

But my favorite energy was and always will be pride. It's a feeling that's always been important to me as a Black person, because when we haven't had anything else, we've had our pride. As James Brown put it so perfectly, "Say It Loud—I'm Black and I'm Proud."

It's the pride in songs like Kendrick Lamar's "Alright"

that helps me keep faith that one day the world will be better for Black people.

> ▶️ Google the lyrics and stream the song; I think you'll understand.

I find the same pride in Solange's song "F.U.B.U.," which is short for "For Us, By Us." The title is very direct, and so is the song itself.

But none of the other lyrics of that song have ever made me feel as strongly as one line, repeated at various points: "Some sh*t is for us."

It's a simple statement, but it has so much meaning behind it. It's a direct response to so many moments in the lives of people—moments when people do things because they don't understand why they can't do them. Even when no one asked them to understand, we just asked them not to do it. Sometimes things shouldn't be done because they're just not meant for you.

The summer before college started, a few friends and I decided to take a road trip upstate to drop off our friend Cynthia (yes, the same Cynthia from earlier), who was starting school early.

It was me, Cynthia, my friend and Cynthia's boyfriend, Carlos (isn't love grand?), our friend Jamel, our friend Dante, and Dante's girlfriend, Tabitha. This was our first time meeting Tabitha, and she seemed nice. She was a young Chinese American woman who met Dante while they were both doing an internship for City Hall.

Like us, Dante was from a poor neighborhood in our city, and he went to school with Carlos. Tabitha went to private school and was not from a neighborhood like ours. But one of the things Dante told us he enjoyed about her was that she never made him feel like they were different.

Since he liked her, we liked her, plus, as soon as we met her, she seemed down-to-earth.

The drive up to Cynthia's school was about four hours one way, so we took Carlos's dad's SUV because it could comfortably fit all of us and had an amazing speaker system.

When we got in the truck, each of us pulled out our iPod to show off our music libraries and decide who would get the aux (be the DJ).

⏮ This was before the age of car Bluetooth and streaming. To play music, you either needed CDs or you had an iPod that stored music that you downloaded. This was when curating music meant a lot, because even those with iPods that could hold a lot of songs were still limited. So music taste really meant something.

After comparing who had the best music selection, it came down to me versus Tabitha to see who was going to have the aux. She had a ton of great music that was very similar to mine, so we decided to let her have it on the way up, since she was the new one in the group.

The pressure was on. We all took having the aux very seriously (and still do). It's not just about putting on a playlist; it's about setting the tone and keeping it. You have to make sure you set the mood and build on that. Everyone has to be consistently happy and excited, or before you know it, your aux privileges are revoked for months.

⏸ I'm happy to say that this has never happened to me. Whether it was on an iPod or now on Spotify, I keep a crowd pleased when I have the aux. If you need someone on the aux for your next event, let me know. I do proms, bar/bat mitzvahs, graduation parties—you name it.

Tabitha didn't fail. She started the road trip strong by playing "Party Like a Rockstar" by the Shop Boyz, which at the time was one of the top songs out. A hit is always a good place to start.

She had the aux for hours, and we heard a mix of everything in that time. Tabitha played new hits and hits we hadn't heard in years that took us back to elementary school with some 98 Degrees. (I already told you my stance on them.) She was rocking.

We were about three hours into the trip when Dante asked Tabitha, "Where's the real rap?" Up to that point, Tabitha had played songs from various genres, many of which were top radio hits, though a few weren't. But when it came to hip-hop and rap, she had played only songs that were on the radio.

She told us she didn't have a lot of non-radio rap songs, but I did. So she gave the aux to me. After playing a few songs by artists like A Tribe Called Quest, Jadakiss, and Mos Def, I realized she didn't know many, if any, of the songs.

⏩ If you don't know these artists, go on whatever streaming service you have and get familiar. This was a different era of rap and hip-hop. For additional recommendations, head on to the back of the book, where I've listed songs in the *Black Friend* Playlist.

Tabitha sat silently in the car and smiled as we bounced around and listened to some of the rap we had grown up on and knew by heart. She looked on, as if wishing she could be involved.

After the rest of us had fun and rapped along for a while, I decided to ask Tabitha if there was a rapper or song she liked that was similar to what I was playing. Before she could respond, Dante said, "Dipset or the Game."

Tabitha responded, "Oh, yeah! All of those guys are cute. I love them."

Dante responded, "Honestly, she knows more of their music than me. We listen to them in her car and she raps along. Watch."

So I picked a song that I figured would be perfect,

because it had both Dipset and the Game featured on it (it was also a favorite of mine): "Certified Gangstas."

As the song started, Dante, Jamel, and I rapped along to the Game's first verse. After the verse, Dante urged Tabitha to rap along. "Watch. Watch. Get 'em, babe!"

Jamel and I stayed silent as the next verse came up so Tabitha could rap along with Jim Jones. She looked at us nervously and then began.

Tabitha rapped along with the swagger of someone performing in front of thousands. We all watched and cheered her on. "Okay! Get 'em, Tabitha!" Jamel yelled.

At a certain point, Jamel and I jumped in to rap as well, because we knew the n-word was coming up in the song and she wouldn't be able to say it.

◼ Again, white readers, I expect you not to say it, either. Especially as it comes up quite a bit in the rest of the story.

A few moments later, the line happened. Jamel and I looked at each other in surprise and confusion. It wasn't just the two of us who had said the line. Tabitha said it as well.

As Tabitha continued rapping and Dante hyped her on as if nothing had happened, Cynthia turned the music down.

"What did you just say?" Cynthia asked.

"What do you mean?" Tabitha responded.

"You just said 'nigga,'" I said.

"So?" Tabitha asked.

Cynthia, Jamel, and I responded at basically the same time.

"The hell?" said Cynthia.

"Oh, nah," said Jamel.

"Get your girl, Dante," I said.

"What's the problem? Dante doesn't care when I say it, and he's Black," Tabitha responded.

We all looked at Dante. Carlos could barely keep his eyes on the road at this point, so he pulled over.

"Dante, you let her say the n-word?" responded Cynthia.

"I mean, yeah. She doesn't call me a nigger with an 'er' or anything. She says it if it's in a song. That's not a big deal," Dante replied.

"It *is* a big deal," Jamel said.

"Why? She's not even white," Dante argued.

"I'm not white, and neither is Cynthia, but we don't say it," Carlos responded.

"But I wouldn't care if you did," Dante said.

"*I* would care if they did, and I'm Black, too," I said.

"So would I," Jamel said.

We sat there on the side of the road for a few minutes, and no one said anything. Eventually Cynthia asked Carlos to turn the car around so we could go back home. She said she didn't want to "bring this type of energy to her new school."

⏮ Cynthia was always like that. She really didn't take any garbage from anyone, as you probably recall from the Halloween brawl we got into the year before.

Carlos turned the car around, and we headed back home. Everyone was still silent for the most part, until Jamel asked Tabitha a question.

"How would you feel if people just wore a bunch of Chinese clothes and took things from Chinese culture but weren't Chinese?" Jamel asked.

"I wouldn't care, and that happens all of the time. Doesn't make any difference," Tabitha responded.

"That's weird," Jamel said. "This white girl in my middle school tried to throw a *Mulan*-themed birthday party at school, and she asked everyone to come wearing 'Chinese fashion.' This Japanese girl in my class got offended, even though it wasn't her specific culture. It turned into a big thing, and the girl had to cancel the party."

"Like I said, that wouldn't make a difference to me. Who cares?" Tabitha said.

"But it should make a difference," Cynthia responded. "It's your culture and your community. You shouldn't just give it away. I don't mind people who are not Latino learning about our cultures, but I don't want people thinking they can just do anything with it."

"We say it, so other people can, too," Dante argued. "It's not that serious."

"We say it because it's ours to say. It's a Black word, and Black people can choose to say it or not," I responded.

Jamel followed my comment by yelling at Dante in frustration, "Yes, it *is* that serious! Because I don't care if you want to let people disrespect you. But I'm not letting just anyone say 'nigga' around me. If you're not Black, don't say it."

"We can have Carlos pull over the car if you want," Dante responded, clearly ready to take this argument to the next level.

"It's whatever to me," Jamel responded.

They took off their seat belts and began moving as if they were ready to fight in the car before it could pull over. I quickly jumped in and told them both to stop.

⏪ The last thing we needed was a car full of young people of color fighting on the highway. It would have been like Christmas morning for some racist police officer.

Everyone stayed absolutely silent for the rest of the ride. We got back, and Carlos dropped Tabitha and Dante off. Before the two got out of the car, Jamel took a quick shot at Dante by saying, "Not all skinfolk are kinfolk."

They stared at each other for a moment, and Dante walked off with Tabitha. It was the last time any of us saw him.

"Not all skinfolk are kinfolk" is something I have heard since I was a child. It's typically used as a slap in the face or to express disappointment in someone. What it basically means is that just because someone looks like you or is part of a community you belong to doesn't mean you are going to share the same values. Especially of the community.

⏪ Another example of when this phrase could have been used was when Kenneth let those two white guys call me a "nigga." I'm not sure if you needed another example, or if I just wanted to remind you how bad Kenneth was; either way, I feel good about it.

That phrase is for those who don't take pride in their community, whatever that community may be. Those who don't understand that "some sh*t is for us."

It's not just about disrespecting clothes or saying words that have a history of a community's pain and struggle. Sometimes "some sh*t is for us" is simply about reflecting, celebrating, hurting, and understanding staying within a community. Because not everything is meant to be shared, especially when some cultures haven't even received the benefit or profits from their culture, while others have.

⏸ One example of this is yoga, which is originally a Hindu tradition. But in America, I'm sure many think it was started by a white woman from Southern California who has a closet full of lululemon workout clothes.

Learning to appreciate that there are things that aren't meant for you takes time for some. It's something I'm still working on myself, and a lesson I was taught in a conversation with someone I admire.

AN INTERVIEW WITH TARELL
ALVIN McCRANEY

*World-renowned actor, playwright, and
Academy Award winner*

I wanted to interview Tarell for the book not just because he's a brilliant artist but also because he changed my life. Tarell is the writer of the play *In Moonlight Black Boys Look Blue*, which became the 2016 Academy Award–winning best picture *Moonlight*.

I saw *Moonlight* in theaters five times, each time bringing a different person with me to make sure they saw it. Every time I watched it, I cried. One of the times, I brought my best friend, and he cried. As a cisgender straight young man, I felt it was the most eye-opening queer story (and story in general) I'd ever seen.

It was such an important story to me that I bought DVDs when it released and gave them as gifts to people at holidays. I felt like Tarell and the director, Barry Jenkins, had spoken to me and other people who weren't in the queer community and showed us why we needed to change, and how alike so many of our stories were.

I would sit in my house and listen to "One Step Ahead" by Aretha Franklin on repeat. It's the only song that plays more than once in the film, and it is used during two pivotal scenes. I'd think about those scenes and others and try to dissect them, my feelings, my understanding, my community.

⏸ I'm actually playing the song on repeat as I write this. Feel free to play it on repeat as you read the rest of this. Rest in peace, Aretha.

The movie brought home to me the idea that all Black people are working to find ourselves, all experiencing pain and joy, regardless of our other identities.

I thought I heard the message loud and clear. But I was wrong, because there was never a message for me to hear, and that's not a bad thing. As we will discuss in a bit.

It was my first time speaking to Tarell, and we were on the phone for about fifteen minutes, discussing things people shouldn't do if they aren't from certain communities. The time was filled with me asking questions and him answering brilliantly.

The entire time I was on the call, I felt like I was back in elementary school, nervous that I would say something to make the popular kid not like me, while also trying not to give away how excited I was about being given a chance to sit at the "cool table."

Tarell then spoke about the power of words such as the

n-word, and whether anyone should be able to use them.

TARELL: Words have power because we endowed them with power. Words, like dollars, don't actually matter until human beings feel that they do or say that they do or socially agree that they do. And so I think a lot of the confusion around certain words and people's cultures or outside of people's cultures and how those words get introduced and how they live and how they're reclaimed or not has a lot to do with where the power lies and who's endowed with that power and who isn't.

There's often a question that is possibly too broad for its own sake. If I tell you, Fred, that you can call me T, then you call me T. You shouldn't call everybody who you meet T. It makes no sense. Therein lies the root of the problem again, in that here's one person taking one person's consent, as it were, or even intimacy, and trying to do the same with a whole people, and that all boils down to power. No, you don't have the power to be intimate with all folks, right? When someone invites you, they have a kind of intimacy to call them outside of their name. That's between you and that person. And in fact, there are times when Black people call each other the n-word and a Black person says, "No, I'm not your n-word," right?

Next, Tarell addressed the issue of people in communities who allow or welcome outsiders to do certain things, when many in the community think they shouldn't have the right. Essentially, the idea of "not all skinfolk are kinfolk."

TARELL: I trust all people to look out for their own self-interests at some point, and when they don't, that's a happy surprise. So I'd rather be happily surprised than shocked at my own understanding of what human nature is. I mean, I can only speak from my experience, but poor Black people have always been politically sophisticated in that way. What I've observed from the elders in the community has always been a distrust of anybody who doesn't live in the community. And even within the community, there are folks who have varying degrees of understanding of what's good for the community, what's not, and that everybody won't be on the same page.

At this point in the interview, I was becoming less nervous and more comfortable. So I decided to pivot the questions to focus on moments when communities created opportunities for outsiders to learn and grow. In reality, it was a selfish question. I wanted to talk about *Moonlight*, and to discuss my appreciation for him creating a story that helped people like me.

Expecting him to say yes, I asked whether *Moonlight* was partially a letter to people outside of the community it was about.

TARELL: Not sure I understand. Was *Moonlight* a letter to people, to not-queer Black people?

ME: To a certain extent. Yeah, yeah, yeah.

TARELL (quickly and firmly): No.

Like a self-centered person, I responded by saying "Really?" demonstrating my surprise that this queer Black man didn't write one of the most important queer Black stories for a young heterosexual Black man.

It took all of two seconds for me to understand how wrong I was. But the deed was done, and Tarell was silent.

⏪ It was at this moment that I felt my heart drop to my shoes, and I started sweating.

TARELL: *Moonlight* was a letter to myself. I wrote *Moonlight* when I was twenty-two years old. My mom had just died, and I needed to remember moments with her and our life. When Barry adapted the original screenplay into *Moonlight*, there's no part of me that didn't know that his central focus was to make a love letter to Liberty City, which is where we both grew up. And all the people, queer or not, who existed there, who lived there, to the crackhead, to the crack-addicted mothers that we both had, to the drug-dealing, surrogate fathers or coaches that we had, to the Kevins, to the Chirons. Certainly he was writing to them. And I think other folks came in and saw that and thought, "Wow, this is a really intimate letter that I'm being let in on." But they weren't the audience; it wasn't for them.

I felt like a complete a**hole. In all my time thinking that I was waving the flag of this story and understood its impact, I didn't realize I was centering myself in someone else's story, someone else's world, someone else's community.

While it meant a lot to me, and even changed me, it wasn't *for* me.

"Some sh*t is just for us."

I gathered the pieces of myself off the floor and asked Tarell a question that I didn't realize would end up creating the second moment in which he changed my life.

I asked Tarell what his thoughts were on the importance of storytelling and how it can help change people's perspectives and lives. Especially in relation to young white people reading this book.

TARELL: I can't really speak to it. I'm not from a white community, and even though I work in and around white people, I rarely see young white people. I hear about what their communities are going through in the newspaper. I don't know their trials and trauma. I've seen *Euphoria*, and maybe that's a window into the suburbs. I don't know. I mean that in the most earnest way that I can, and that I don't engage in that way. However, I will say that the purpose for storytelling for me, and what I try to do, is specific.

I walk out of the door and most times I'm in a neighborhood now that doesn't look like me. So the first story I'm being told is I'm alone.

And then I'm socialized through that the whole day, and then I kind of fight really hard—and they don't even know that I'm fighting really hard—with people to make them understand my point of view. Make sure I'm heard, make sure I'm treated with the delicacy and the kind of roughness that is needed in my community for growth. And that's exhausting. So I tell stories for people like me. It feels good to sit in a room and sit down in front of an MBJ [Michael B. Jordan] film or television show. It feels good to sit down and go, yes, yes. To be reminded that I do exist. I'm reminded that there is a community that comes from a place like me. Even if it's not exact. I'm reminded, I'm allowed to know, that I am not alone and that I do exist. Those are the stories I want to tell.

Tarell helped me understand two things. One: Whether it's clothing, foods, words, anything, it's important that people not only understand that some things are *historically* off-limits to noncommunity members, but that "some sh*t is just for us" also means creating new sh*t sometimes that belongs to the community.

Which leads me to the second thing I came to understand: Like our foods, words, and clothing, our stories are also ours to keep in our communities as we decide to do. Our traumas, our struggles, our joys—they are ours. This book is part of not only my story, but my community's story.

Tarell's story wasn't for me, and like many other things, it didn't have to be. Maybe it's best that it wasn't. That doesn't mean I can't watch it, enjoy it, and learn from it. It means that it was made with a very specific community in mind, to make them feel seen, to help them feel loved.

It's a testament to how powerful Tarell's story is: even being on the outside looking in, I still learned to love a community more than I did before and in the process became a better person. Which is the same thing I often want for people who aren't from my communities, people like many of you.

Just because it isn't yours doesn't mean you can't still treat it with love and care.

I actually had another revelation while talking to Tarell. (That's three, for those keeping score.) The idea of doing things for your own community made me want to make a point to my white readers that I haven't made yet.

While this book is meant to be a guide for white people to understand and be better, it's important that white people also understand that it isn't the duty of Black people or people of color to explain things. I'm doing so because I hope it can ultimately make change for my community.

But it's important to understand that this book is a gift, not an obligation.

The gift is in the form of an opportunity. It's an opportunity that I thought was my duty to give, but it's not.

That's what makes this book special. It's an opportunity to learn, grow, and share where many may otherwise never have the chance.

It's me hoping that you'll understand and appreciate that much of what you're reading is normally some sh*t that's just for us.

IN THE END

WE DON'T NEED ALLIES; WE NEED ACCOMPLICES

■ We're friends now. Well, at least, I'm hoping we are.

I think people become friends by sharing moments. By laughing together, hurting together, learning together. I feel like by this point in the book we've done that.

I've shared some of the worst moments of my life with you, and some of the best. All in an effort for you to learn to trust me. Because when there's trust between friends, they can have hard conversations.

We've had some of those conversations already, as I and other people I know have been talking about how white people can be better. But the conversation we are about to have is probably the most difficult.

This conversation is about *making* change instead of just *wanting* change. As the chapter title says, being accomplices instead of allies—which is a concept that I first heard used by author and activist Mikki Kendall.

Merriam-Webster defines an ally as "someone that aligns with and supports a cause with another individual or group of people."

This is someone whose friend is a person of color. One day they are in class, and one of the white students uses a racial slur toward their friend. They feel bad, but they watch and do nothing. Later they ask their friend if they are okay.

Merriam-Webster defines an accomplice as "a person who knowingly, voluntarily, or intentionally gives assistance to another in the commission of a crime."

Now, I'm not asking you to commit crimes. I'm asking you to focus on the first part of that definition: "a person who knowingly, voluntarily, or intentionally gives assistance to another."

An accomplice is a person who actively participates in some way.

This is someone whose friend is a person of color. One day they are in class, and one of the white students uses a racial slur toward their friend. They know it's wrong, so they decide to do something about it. They might step in and say something to defend their friend, tell a teacher or administrator about the incident, or let their parents know and ask them to do something.

This is the difference between someone who is hoping for change and someone who is trying to make change. An ally versus an accomplice.

I'm asking you to be an accomplice. I'm asking you to make change for the boy in the stories you've been reading about, and so many children like him.

That's why I wrote this book, why so many people agreed to share their thoughts, and why I wanted us to become friends—for change.

Not just for white people to change, but for all of us to change. I had to change from high school to college, and from college to adulthood. From being a hurt and confused boy to a man trying to figure out how to stop the things that hurt and confused me from happening to others.

During those times, I've grown frustrated, tired, and angry. That was often the sum of my experiences you've read about, and many others': anger.

I think we deserve to be angry. As you've read, it would be an extreme understatement to say that being a Black person in society is hard.

There aren't words that can explain the generations of trauma and pain that Black people continue to deal with, not just in this country but around the world.

Much of the same could be said for people of color from almost any group.

People like me who have dealt with enough trauma to last a lifetime before they were a teenager. People whose parents and grandparents dealt with all of that and worse. People who are tired and have every right to be.

For so long we have fought and lost not only our battles but also our lives, while just trying to create a world where people of color are treated fairly and equally.

Yet here we are, still dealing with many of the same issues, and some worse than ever. Being tired is understandable.

Many people have asked me why I was even writing this book. Some have called it pointless and a waste of my time when I could be "making actual change." Honestly, there have been times when I've felt the same way.

When I started this book, I asked myself one question: "If I show people how they're hurting others, will some of them be willing to change?"

There have been many times while writing this book that the answer was no. Times when people have gone online and called me a nigger or threatened my family. Just because I want better for people who are tired.

But I kept writing. Because frankly, I don't know what else to do. This book isn't filled with new conversations, new ideas, or an academic analysis. I didn't want it to be.

All I wanted was to talk to you, and let you get to know me, and see if you were open to being friends. Because friends not only hear each other; they listen.

I've already lived through the moments that you've read about, and countless others that you haven't. But my little brother hasn't, my niece hasn't, and neither have the children I hope to have one day (but am also scared to have one day).

They are the reason I wanted you to listen to me. The reason I'm asking you to help me make change.

The reason I have one more story for you. A story that I haven't told anyone.

A story for my friend, to help you understand the importance of being an accomplice.

. . . .

I've known I was Black since I was a kid. Once I started observing the world, it was hard not to know. For better or worse, my world was different. I was treated differently from my classmates, my family was different from the families I saw on TV, and I had to act differently from how I saw other kids acting in public.

My mother and grandmother also made sure I knew I was different.

I didn't understand why they had to tell me I was a Black kid every time I pretended to play cops and robbers with an imaginary gun. Why they'd ask if I understood what Black kids couldn't do when we'd see white kids play pranks on strangers. Why they'd make sure I remembered that police weren't always nice to Black kids, and to stay still and be silent if I was around them.

I didn't know why things were different for Black kids; I just knew they were, and I hated it.

I respected my mother and grandmother, so I listened to what they told me, but like any child, I also tried to get away with what I could.

Most of the times that I did things I was told not to, it was because I was trying to fit in. It was hard enough being an unpopular kid, but being an unpopular kid who also couldn't be careless and fun made other kids like me even less.

Which is why by the time elementary school was over, I was tired of being unpopular, tired of being bullied, tired of being alone.

The beginning of middle school started pretty much the same as elementary school had gone.

I was still me, and kids still treated me like crap for being me.

But middle school was worse than anything I had dealt with, because it wasn't just about being dorky anymore. We were all about eleven years old, and now kids were starting to judge one another by new things, like attractiveness and how much money your family had.

Based on how my level of bullying increased, I guess I was poorer and uglier than I was dorky.

But there was a silver lining, as in my first week of school, I finally made two friends: Ryan and Marcus.

Ryan was a young white kid who had just moved to Yonkers from New Jersey after his father had passed away.

His mom was now raising him and his siblings as a single parent, and she didn't have much money. They lived in one of Yonkers's low-income areas, which I had never seen a white person do.

Marcus was pretty similar to me: a Black kid who didn't have much, stayed out of people's way, loved being a nerd, and someone who girls didn't think was cute.

The three of us met in the cafeteria. Ryan and I didn't know each other, but we each saw the other nervously looking for a place to sit. Ryan decided to come over to me and ask whether I had a suggestion. Marcus saw us searching aimlessly and invited us to the "safe zone" table. (Yes, the same one mentioned earlier.)

After that day, we became great friends. But having one another didn't change the fact that we were all bullied constantly, which is why a lot of our time was spent figuring out how to be bullied less.

It seemed like an impossible task, until one day after school when Marcus's older sister took us to a local sneaker store with her to look at things we couldn't afford.

> ⏮ Marcus's sister, Vanessa, went to a high school that was about five minutes away from our school. So she'd pick us up sometimes and let us hang out with her. Marcus had told us that she wasn't very popular in her school, which is probably why she was nice to us; she felt our pain.

While we were in the store, a group of older popular girls from our school walked in. The store was small, so the girls saw us, but they didn't acknowledge our presence. Which was a lot better than how they treated us in school. The girls seemed to know exactly what they wanted, because they came in and were quickly at the register and on their way out.

As they were leaving, we overhead one of the girls say that she wanted a shirt that she saw, but her mother hadn't given her enough money for it. After they left, Ryan told us he was going to steal the shirt and give it to the girl at school the next day. He figured it would be a way to get on their good side.

Ryan waited until all of the staff at the store were preoccupied, looked for a blind spot on the cameras, and stuffed the shirt in his coat.

Not only was I in shock; I was nervous beyond description. I had always been taught that stealing was one of the worst things I could ever do. Which is why Ryan and Marcus had to basically drag me out of the store, because I was afraid to leave with them and the shirt.

The next day at school, we went up to the girls in the cafeteria and Ryan gave them the shirt. They were stunned.

While we were standing there, one of the older guys who had also been bullying us saw us talking to the girls and said, "Y'all are too ugly to be talking to them. How about you—"

Before he could continue, the girl who the shirt was for said, "Shut up and stop bothering us."

⏮ I'm not sure what we expected to happen, but it couldn't have been as good as what actually happened. An older popular girl protected us, which was about as good as having a parade held for us.

After the guy walked away, the girls asked us if we could get them some more clothes, so we did. Over the next few weeks, we stole clothes, lip gloss, makeup, and anything else they wanted.

We would go to the mall and wait until security and store staff were distracted and steal items in our coats and book bags where cameras couldn't see us.

But we never stole anything for ourselves. We were just trying to keep the girls happy, since they were defending us from bullies and making other kids start to treat us differently because they saw the girls speaking to us.

I'm not sure how long we thought we could keep it all going. But I guess we were prepared to do it for the foreseeable future if it meant surviving at school.

I stayed home from school one day because I wasn't feeling well. My mother had to go to work, so my grandmother came over to take care of me.

While at my house, my grandmother decided to clean up my room a bit. As she was cleaning, my book bag fell on the floor. All of the things I had recently stolen and had planned on taking to school that day came tumbling out.

There were hair supplies, makeup, and costume jewelry all over the floor.

My grandmother looked at me in shock and asked, "How did you get these? Where did you get these from?" I didn't respond; I knew this was going to be bad.

She followed up with the same questions again, this time yelling. She must have seen my face turn pale and knew. A few seconds later, she grabbed my shirt and looked me in my eyes and asked slowly, "Did you steal these?"

I remained silent, because I didn't know what to say. I didn't want to lie to my grandmother, but I also knew telling her the truth was going to break her heart and get me in trouble. She then pulled me closer and yelled, "Frederick, did you steal these?"

In a soft voice I quickly responded, "Yes."

As soon as the word left my mouth, my grandmother slapped me and went to sit at the edge of my bed and started crying.

⏮ This is the only time I can remember my grandmother hitting me, other than lightly slapping my hand when I was disobedient as a child.

She began speaking to herself and praying, "Lord, please, not my grandson. Let us figure this out. Let us find a way." It was in that moment that I realized she wasn't angry; she was afraid.

I apologized to her and then told her all about the kids at school and explained why I had been stealing with my friends.

"You and Marcus are going to get yourselves in trouble. None of you should be stealing, but if you get caught, Ryan won't be dealing with the same things," she responded.

I asked her whether she was going to tell my mother, and she agreed not to as long as I promised never to do it again. I looked her in her eyes and I promised.

> ⏪ That was the first and last time I ever lied to my grandmother.

My grandmother thought about having me return the stolen items but figured that the store owners might not be understanding and might call the police. Instead, she decided to place the items in a trash bag and take it with her to throw away later.

> ⏸ I actually learned recently that many white people that I know stole from stores as children, but they never had to worry about the same consequences as children of color do. For many white people, it's a normal childhood mistake, not potentially life altering.

The next day at school when we went to give the girls their latest items, I was the only one who didn't have anything to give them. One of the girls said, "Well, then, there's no reason to know you, ugly." Then they quickly began making fun of me.

Just like that, weeks of peace gone in a moment. I was frantic and refused to go back to being treated like garbage.

"I'll have more later this week!" I said.

The girls stopped, and Ryan and Marcus stared at me, looking both confused and nervous. I had told them what happened with my grandmother, and they both said I should stop.

The girl who had called me ugly said, "Well, if that's the case, maybe you aren't that ugly. See you Wednesday!" Then they walked away.

Ryan and Marcus told me I was making a mistake and shouldn't do it, but I refused to go back to being bullied. I couldn't take it.

The following day after school, we asked Vanessa whether Ryan and I could go to the mall with her. (Marcus couldn't come because he had a dentist appointment.)

She told us she wasn't going to the mall we typically went to near school, that she had decided to go to the Westchester mall with some of her friends.

⏪ The Westchester mall was in upper Westchester and, as opposed to those in the mall we normally went to, most of the stores were luxury. Most of the people who went there were wealthy and white, as upper Westchester was generally. I often heard people say they didn't like going there because they felt the staff at stores and security were racist.

As always, she told us to be careful and to meet her at the food court in an hour. We agreed and looked for stores that we thought would have the best items for the girls and little security.

We found a store with a young staff, various things that we would typically steal, and, most important, no security.

As soon as we went into the store, we waited for the staff to be busy and got started. We stuffed our coats with earrings, bracelets, scrunchies, anything we could find that wouldn't be easily seen.

When we were done, we checked to make sure that no one was looking and headed toward the door. First went Ryan, and I was next. He watched from outside the store as I slowly made my way toward the door so as not to draw attention to myself.

As I turned the handle on the door and began to open it, the door was pushed shut. "Oh, no, you don't."

I turned around to see a tall white man in a hoodie, jeans, and a baseball cap. He yanked my arm and began pulling me along with him.

"Get off of me!" I yelled. At which point another man

came over. He was also white and wearing a baseball cap, and he had on a tracksuit.

"Another one of those little punks stealing stuff," the man holding me said to him.

I yelled again, "Stop grabbing me! Get off of me!"

The man in the tracksuit ignored me. "Where'd this one put the stuff?"

The man holding me responded, "In his coat."

The man in the tracksuit then grabbed me, unzipped my coat, and forcefully pulled it off me, hurting my arm in the process. He then started pulling out all the items I'd stolen.

I realized that they were undercover security guards, and I felt my stomach drop. I stared at the door, looking to see if Ryan was going to help me.

The man in the hoodie saw me looking at Ryan, so he opened the door and asked, "Do you know this kid?"

Ryan looked at me for a second, then said no. He then walked away slowly and didn't turn back. The security guard closed the door and walked back over to me.

As soon as I saw Ryan leave, my heart began racing. I started shaking and then crying.

The two men pulled me toward the side of the register in the store and placed the items I'd stolen on the counter.

The man in the tracksuit laughed and said, "Oh, now you want to cry?"

I just stared at him and continued crying louder. Customers began to watch the scene.

The man in the hoodie asked how old I was. Through my crying, I told him I was eleven years old. He got frustrated and said, "So you want to steal stuff and then lie? This is the problem with you people."

"I'm eleven, I swear," I responded. I was small for my age and was used to people thinking I was younger than I was.

But what he said next was "You're obviously older than that!"

⏸ I didn't know it at the time, but there's a long history in this country of **white people assuming Black children are older than they are**—sometimes with deadly consequences for those same children.

I kept crying and said, "I swear I'm eleven."

"You have the nerve to lie to my face? You can lie to the police, then!" He grabbed my arm again and pulled me with so much force that I hit one of the clothing racks and fell with it.

While I was on the floor, I heard someone say, "He's just a kid! Relax!" and another say, "Don't do that to him!"

But no one stepped in.

While I was on the floor, I wasn't able to catch my breath, and I could feel my heart pounding throughout my body. I couldn't move at all. I didn't know what was happening to me, but I was terrified.

The two security guards kept yelling for me to get up, but I couldn't.

"Stop trying to make a scene, you a**hole!" one of them yelled. A moment later, the man in the hoodie snatched me and pulled me to my feet, but I couldn't stand and immediately fell back down.

I was breathing so heavily that people started walking over to see what was happening.

"Is he okay?" I heard a man say.

"He's fine. He's trying to make a scene because he got caught stealing!" one of the security guards responded.

The man who asked whether I was okay then said, "I'm a doctor and he doesn't look okay. I think he's having a panic attack. Get him some water."

One of the security guards responded, "He doesn't need—"

The man cut him off: "Get this kid some damn water!"

The man then helped me to sit up and told me to breathe slowly.

He was a well-dressed young white man wearing slacks, a sweater, and a tan trench coat.

"Breathe slowly," he said again. Moments later, the security guard in the tracksuit handed the man water, and he gave it to me and told me to drink it and continue to breathe. I began to calm down.

"What's your name?" the man asked.

"Frederick," I responded.

"That's a good name. I'm Brian," he said.

I asked him what his last name was. "It's Owens, but you can just call me Brian."

"Thank you, Mr. Owens. My mother said I can't call adults by their first name," I replied. I finished the cup of water and looked around and saw customers and the security guards staring.

Brian smiled and said, "You seem like a respectful kid. Did your mother also tell you not to steal, Frederick?"

"Yes," I said.

"So, why are you stealing?" Brian asked.

"It was for the girls in school who bully me," I confessed.

"I remember those days. How old are you?" Brian asked.

"I swear I'm eleven," I responded.

A second later, the man in the hoodie looked at the door and said, "Perfect—the cops are here. Let's get him out of here." At that point I began crying again.

Two older white police officers came in and asked what was going on. The security guards told them they had caught me stealing and showed them all the items that they had found in my coat.

"They always come here to steal. Wish they'd stay in their own mall," one of the officers said, and then he looked at me and told me to get up.

Brian helped me to my feet while I continued crying.

The officer then put his hand on my shoulder and said, "All right, come on, let's go."

Before I could move, Brian held me back and asked the police officers where they were taking me. They told him I was going to go down to the security office while they filed paperwork and then would be taken to the precinct.

"He's just a kid—is all of that necessary? He's obviously shaken up, I'm sure he won't do this again," Brian responded.

"He's a thief. If he didn't want it to come to this, he shouldn't have stolen anything. That's what these types of kids do," the officer responded.

"What do you mean 'these types of kids'?" Brian asked.

The officer ignored him and told me to "come on." So I followed him and the other officer toward the door.

I had never been more afraid in my life. Everything my mother and grandmother had taught me, I'd ignored. I knew they couldn't help me after this.

As the officer opened the door, Brian yelled, "I forgot to pay for the stuff!"

I turned around to look at him, as did the officers.

"What?" said one of the officers.

Brian continued: "I should have said something already, but I was nervous. Sorry, everyone. He didn't steal anything. I forgot to pay. He was helping me pick things for my daughter's birthday. I'll pay for everything now. You can let him go."

I was beyond confused. Why was this white man lying for me?

"He's lying, officer! He doesn't even know him!" the security guard in the hoodie objected.

"His name is Frederick, he's eleven, and he's a good kid. Let him go," Brian said.

"This is why these black kids never learn. They act like thugs and never deal with any consequences," the guard in the hoodie said.

"Thugs? He's a *kid*. Is that why you attacked an eleven-year-old and cut his arm?" Brian pointed at the blood running down my arm that I hadn't realized was there.

"Maybe you want to explain that to the news?" Brian continued. "How about you, officers? A white man asks an eleven-year-old kid to help him pick out birthday presents, and security decides to assault him, and the police arrest him. Even though the white man admitted it was his mistake."

The officers and security guards looked at one another for a second, and then one officer took his hand off my shoulder, looked at me, and said, "Get the hell out of here, kid."

I looked at Brian as the officer approached him, and I began to say, "He didn't—"

Brian cut me off, pulled out his wallet, and said, "It's okay. Go." I didn't move.

"Go!" Brian said again more firmly.

I began to walk toward the exit. Before I left, Brian yelled, "Frederick!"

I turned around, and he said, "Don't forget to listen to

your mother!" Then one of the officers pushed me through the door.

Once I was out of the store, I ran from the mall. I didn't bother going to the food court and finding Ryan or Vanessa. I ran to a bus stop and waited there, crying until a bus pulled up, and then I sat on the bus and cried until I got home, the whole time thinking about what I had just done, how close I had come to undoing everything I had been taught.

I never told anyone what had happened. I also never explained to Ryan what happened after he ran, but I stopped being friends with him.

I didn't expect him to take the fall for me like Brian did, or put himself in harm's way. But he left me like I was nothing.

I never saw Brian again, though I thought about what he did for me for a long time. But I didn't really understand it until I got older.

What I did was wrong. But it seemed that Brian understood the bigger picture. Because I was Black, I wasn't being treated as if I was a kid who had made a mistake.

I wasn't a thug, a thief, a liar, or an a**hole. I was just an eleven-year-old kid who made a mistake because he was tired of being bullied.

Unlike the other customers in the store, Brian didn't just stand by and watch these white men derail my life because of a mistake; he used his privilege to do the right thing. He decided to be an accomplice; he decided to make a change.

Another thing I've considered as I've gotten older is that there was no reward or public merit for Brian's actions. He wasn't attempting to be a **white savior**—he seemingly just wanted to do the right thing.

That moment helped me understand exactly why my mother and grandmother feared for my life. Why they wouldn't let me pretend to play with guns. Why they held me close whenever police walked by.

Because Black kids don't get to make mistakes. Black kids don't get to be kids. Black kids get judgment and bullets.

Remember when I said I was scared to have children of my own? It's because bringing Black children into the world means there will be another generation thrown into a toxic society filled with daily microaggressions. It means they will have a life filled with tragic moments fueled by racism. Moments such as the first time they learn what the word "nigger" means.

Black children have to lose their innocence before white children do. They can't afford the luxury of just reading about the impact of racism and white supremacy in a book, because they're living it every day. Because oftentimes it means life or death.

These children aren't alone. In this country and around the world, generation after generation, children of color are having to carry the weight of survival, simply because they aren't white.

This was the case with me when my mother sat me down and explained why some people would treat me poorly throughout my life because I didn't look like them. I was about eight years old at the time.

These are the same conversations I've been having with my younger brother. Conversations about being Black. Conversations about history. Conversations about racism. Conversations about survival.

He's eight years old.

My brother is the same age I was when I started having these conversations, and some may think they are too early. But Tamir Rice was only a few years older than him when he was murdered by police officer Timothy Loehmann. Tamir was described as looking "like an adult," as "looking vicious," as being "frightening." He was a twelve-year-old *child*. He was a baby. Now he's gone.

Our children don't get to just be children, don't get to just be innocent. The weight of the world is on our children, and it's crucial that we teach them to hold it.

I've been watching as my brother learns about the world around him, and as he does, his innocence slowly leaves his eyes and his spirit, replaced by fear and caution. It breaks my heart, but it must be done. Because I love him, because I know innocence won't protect him. The same way it didn't protect me.

Which is part of why I said no when I asked myself, "If I show people how they're hurting others, will some of them be willing to change?" Because writing about these moments in this book *hurt*. And hearing others' stories about similar or worse moments *hurt*. As I've written this book, I've ached and grieved for myself and for others.

Eventually that pain turned into fear and doubt. Because when you've been hurt time and time again by others, it can be damn hard to believe that anyone actually cares. That anything—or anyone—can or will actually change.

I began to tell myself that people might not change for the better even if I used examples from my personal experiences and life. I feared that the pain of Black people and people of color might not matter to anyone but us. I nearly defeated the idea of this book before even giving it a chance.

But along the way, I realized that if I don't believe the answer is yes, then, as many people said, this is pointless. And if this is pointless, then I don't have a way of making a change for my brother.

Which is why I've asked you to get to know me, hoping you'll let me be the friend that you might not have. The person who tells you what not to do and why you shouldn't do it. The type of person more of us need in our lives.

Friendship also means trust, and that's why I've been honest with you. Honest about my pain, my fears, my mistakes, and my hopes. Because I trust you, it also means I believe in you.

I believe that after getting to know me, you'll be the

friend to someone else that I've been to you. You'll remind people when they do something wrong that it's not okay, and you'll step in to be an accomplice when the moment calls for it. You'll take a look at yourself and find the courage not to hurt people the way you have in the past, and the way others have done and continue to do.

I trust you, and that's why I'll be honest and tell you that change is not easy. For some people, it won't matter that we're friends, or that you're friends with people who are like me.

Those are the people who won't see us. It's those people who will require us to have courage in our friendship.

To those people, it won't matter that I used to hold my brother with one arm when he was an infant, that he would cry when I would leave, that he loves video games, or that his favorite food is chicken tenders. It won't matter that he's sweet and likes to give people hugs so they know he cares.

It won't matter, because they won't see my brother. The same way they didn't see Michael Brown, Tamir Rice, Trayvon Martin, Emmett Till, and countless children of color just like them.

They are the same people who didn't want to see me.

They will see what my teachers saw, what the parents of my friends saw, what my classmates saw, what those security guards saw, what the police saw. They will see whatever they want to see and whatever they expect to see.

But you're nothing like them, and that's exactly why we're friends.

▶ I wouldn't be me if I didn't tell you to listen to something to close us out. Let's end this with "Umi Says" by Mos Def.

"Shine your light on the world …"

Until next time.

Your friend,

Fred

AN ENCYCLOPEDIA OF RACISM

This encyclopedia features concepts from the book that I thought might need to be expanded on. Basically, I've saved you the hassle of googling. You're welcome.

AFFIRMATIVE ACTION

As I've mentioned throughout the book, inequality is built into every aspect of American society, giving Black and brown people less access than white people to education, employment, and power. (See the **white privilege** entry for more on this.)

In 1961, President Kennedy's administration developed a program to help ensure fairness in government hiring and coined the term "affirmative action" to describe it.

Affirmative action has been used to inform things such as college admissions and equal employment opportunity programs. It's based on the notion that "neutral" hiring practices are not enough to fix the historic inequality; institutions need to take action to analyze practices, identify stumbling blocks, and seek out diverse candidates.

ALL LIVES MATTER

"All Lives Matter" is a phrase that started being used in response to the **Black Lives Matter** movement. Black Lives Matter is a call to action for Black people to no longer be murdered by white racists and to receive equal treatment under the law. In response, All Lives Matter aims to say that everyone should matter equally—but ignores and rejects the lived experiences of Black people.

While the "All Lives" notion of equality may make sense to some, it inherently continues the status quo and the injustices Black people face. This is part of the reason that the phrase has been adopted by many white supremacist groups in an attempt to invalidate the importance of Black trauma and murders.

BLACK HAIR

There is a great deal of history when it comes to Black hair. On the surface, it may seem as simple as the fact that most Black people have a different hair texture and, often, styles from other racial groups. But that hair texture and those hair styles cause Black women and men to be treated differently from other people. From people asking to touch our hair to not having products made for our hair texture, Black people have to struggle with racist moments and **microaggressions** because of hair.

These are moments that a white person would likely

never have to face. Touching someone is an invasion of privacy, and assuming you have the right to touch someone is a demonstration of the inequality between Black people and white people. Our people have been killed because of a look we may (or may not!) have given a white person, yet a white person feels they can reach out and touch our hair? That is deeply messed up.

Historically, Black people have also used certain styles such as braids to help with survival. For instance, during slavery and other periods, some Black people would hide grains and other small foods in their braids to help sustain themselves when owners of enslaved people would not feed them. (For more on this, visit: https://www.essence.com/hair/african-braiding-technique-rice-hunger-slavery/.)

This is a reason there tends to be frustration from the Black community when other groups wear hairstyles such as braids that have historical context and significance for us. In addition, Black people are often censured for wearing Black hairstyles while white people who appropriate these styles may not be.

BLACK LIVES MATTER

Black Lives Matter (BLM) is a movement, phrase, and hashtag started by Alicia Garza, Patrisse Cullors, and Opal Tometi as a direct response to consistent violence and racism against Black people. The movement gained popularity and support in 2013 and 2014 after the acquittal of

George Zimmerman in the murder of Trayvon Martin and the murders of Eric Garner and Michael Brown by the police. Its message and call to action are simple: in the face of Black people's lives being carelessly taken, society should be forced to understand that the lives of Black people matter.

BLACK PANTHER

Black Panther is a 2018 American superhero film based on the Marvel Comics character of the same name. It was Marvel Studios' first Black-led film, their first film with a Black director, and their first with a predominantly Black cast. It became the first comic-book superhero film to be nominated for best picture at the Academy Awards.

BREXIT

The United Kingdom was once a member of the European Union (EU), but in 2016, a slim majority of UK citizens voted to withdraw from the EU, largely due to widespread **xenophobia** and a political campaign based on misinformation and fear. The term *Brexit* comes from the words *British* and *exit*.

COLOR BLINDNESS

Color blindness is when people say they "don't see race," which is impossible, as the concept of race was designed to be something people could see. How else would you know whom to give power to and whom to enslave?

People who claim to be color-blind are attempting to express that they don't have racist attitudes or thoughts as an individual—but fail to realize that this does more harm than good. What they are actually doing is choosing not to be uncomfortable, not understanding that even if they don't take issue with other races, many do. The only way to actually make a change is to acknowledge and support someone else's experiences due to their race, not ignore them.

Some might argue that color blindness began as a utopian goal—an effort to treat everyone equally, regardless of race. But it quickly turned into an excuse for many, especially white people, to deny that race is a factor in everything from discriminatory government policies; unequal treatment by law enforcement; voter suppression; access to jobs, goods, and services; and on and on.

By ignoring the role race plays in these issues, you are guaranteeing that nothing will change for those being oppressed or disproportionately impacted. Ultimately, "color-blind" simply means turning a blind eye to the problems faced by people of color.

CULTURAL APPROPRIATION

Cultural appropriation is when a person adopts elements from a culture outside their own. This can include fashion, speech patterns or accents, hairstyles, physical features, and styles or trends. Cultural appropriation is often done by a dominant culture appropriating a disadvantaged culture.

EDUCATIONAL SYSTEM

In America, our educational system was developed by white people, and still today, most of the decision makers are white. Thus, often what and how we learn in school is through a white lens.

In most schools, students don't learn about the history of people of color in America other than during a designated month, and the history we are taught is often biased in favor of white people. For instance, from an early age we learn about Europeans coming to America but rarely about the genocide and trauma they inflicted upon the indigenous peoples.

Another example is that we learn about very few historical figures of color in America who have had a deep impact on our country. I mention some important people of color throughout the book, but also check out the list of "People to Learn More About" on pages 255–257. Every one of these figures should be taught in American schools, but most are not.

THE EVENING NEWS

The news, whether on television, on the radio, or in print, has historically been one of the most dangerous tools in the racist depictions of Black and brown people. Many people take the news as the ultimate truth. Unfortunately, many news outlets cover or tell stories that present Black people in a negative light—as criminals and dangers to society. This builds a narrative and false understanding in the minds of many white people about Black people. Many people have used this false narrative to incite fear in white people and ultimately get them to make decisions based on that fear.

One example of this happened during former president Ronald Reagan's "War on Drugs." His administration used the news and other media to build a false narrative that drugs were a major issue in America that was threatening American lives more than ever, and the main place for drugs was in was Black communities. None of that was true.

But the fear that the narrative created in white people allowed him to take action through laws and policing that devastatingly impacted Black and brown communities and helped further the system of **mass incarceration**.

I suggest watching Ava DuVernay's documentary *13th* on the prison industrial complex and America's history of **systemic racism** to learn more.

HISTORICALLY BLACK COLLEGES AND UNIVERSITIES (HBCUs)

HBCUs are colleges and universities established before the Civil Rights Act of 1964 to primarily serve the African-American community. Like most places in America, higher education institutions had been historically segregated or simply didn't allow African Americans to attend. The creation of HBCUs was not only a way to help grant access to higher education for African Americans; it also helped ensure a safe space to pursue education.

There is a great deal of culture, tradition, and history rooted in HCBUs that has had widespread impact, and I suggest learning more about these institutions. You might want to start by watching *A Different World*.

INTERSECTION

The theory of intersectionality was developed by Kimberlé Crenshaw. An intersection is a point where two or more things meet. The way I've used the term in the book is to help readers understand that a person's life is not constrained to one identity or experience. Multiple things can be true about a person at one time, including the oppression they face. For instance, Black women suffer from sexism, as do white women. But they also suffer from racism, because they're Black. Meaning their experiences live at the intersection of racism and sexism.

MAINSTREAM

Mainstream is another word for popular, but it focuses on the appeal to widespread masses and is used in reference to music, movies, TV shows, and other aspects of pop culture. Things tend to become mainstream based on influential cultures and people. Most things that are mainstream in

America are things that appeal to white people because the people deciding what gets made are predominantly white.

MASS INCARCERATION

The United States has the largest prison population in the world, both in total and per capita. And a disproportionate number of those imprisoned are Black: according to the Pew Research Center, in 2017, African Americans accounted for 33 percent of the incarcerated population despite making up only 12 percent of the total adult population.

Black people are incarcerated at more than *five times* the rate of white people.

When slavery was outlawed, states turned to mass incarceration as a means of using forced labor to increase the profits of business and individuals. And *again*, I suggest watching Ava DuVernay's *13th* to learn much more.

MELTING POT

"Melting pot" is a term used to describe a society made up of people from various races, genders, religions, and other identities where cultural exchange is taking place. One of the first things we learn about America in school is this melting pot concept, the idea that we are all here working and living well together. Ultimately, not only is that not true; it also lets white people escape accountability for creating systems and moments to separate everyone else from white people.

Instead of the melting pot image, I see America as more of a tray of food where everything is on the same tray but the foods don't mix with one another. We are all here, but it doesn't mean we are together.

MICROAGGRESSION

Merriam-Webster covers it pretty well here, defining *microaggression* as "a comment or action that subtly and often unconsciously or unintentionally expresses a prejudiced attitude toward a member of a marginalized group."

MOST PEOPLE LIVING IN POVERTY IN AMERICA ARE WHITE

It's a widely held belief that most people living in poverty in America are nonwhite, but this is false. While percentages of people living in poverty are high within communities of color, most Americans who are living in poverty are white. (Learn more here: https://www.census.gov/library/publications /2018/demo/p60-263.html.)

#OSCARSSOWHITE

#OscarsSoWhite was created by activist April Reign in 2015, a year when many were critical of the lack of nominations and wins for people of color at the Academy Awards when there were many films and actors of color thought to be worthy.

The film *Selma*, for example, was nominated for an Academy Award for best picture, but its director, Ava DuVernay, and leading actor, David Oyelowo, were not nominated for their roles. For the first time since 1998, all twenty contenders for lead and supporting actors were white.

The #OscarsSoWhite movement helped fuel conversations not only about the Academy Awards but also about the lack of representation and accolades for people of color in Hollywood more generally.

#REPRESENTATIONMATTERS

#RepresentationMatters is a movement based on the idea that people from marginalized communities (including people of color, indigenous people, LGBTQIA+ folks, and women) should have the opportunity to see positive representations of themselves in media and art. By doing so, there is a greater likelihood that they will be successful and be treated by others in ways that acknowledge their full humanity.

STEREOTYPE

A stereotype is a set of assumptions or beliefs about a group of people. A stereotype can be of a racial group, an ethnicity, a nationality, or any category of people. Stereotypes underlie and reinforce bigoted attitudes and oppression. Even stereotypes that appear harmless on the surface are a way of saying someone is an "other" and of failing to respect or see people as individuals, and therefore potentially contributing to prejudice and harm.

SYSTEMIC OR INSTITUTIONAL RACISM

Systemic or institutional racism is a kind of stealth racism. It's the reinforcement of white supremacy through various strategies, plans, and parts of everyday life. It's the inequality that is built into our laws, our economic system, our criminal justice system, our housing system, our health care system, our educational system, our entertainment. As I said, it exists in just about every single thing you can think of.

But just because it exists in everything doesn't mean it's obvious. The stealth nature of systemic racism is what makes it so dangerous. A good example is the disproportionate impact of COVID-19 on Black communities, and the coverage of it in the media.

The early narrative had been that Black and brown people are more susceptible to COVID-19 due to weakened immune systems because of health issues such as diabetes and heart disease. But that narrative failed to include the historic factors in why many Black people suffer from certain conditions.

By design of those in power, many Black people have generationally lived in neighborhoods that don't have access to healthy food options. Many Black people also have been placed in financial constraint due to lack of employment opportunities, which in turn often means no access to health care. These are just two examples from a long list of reasons COVID-19 isn't randomly impacting Black people more; rather, systemic racism has made the Black community more vulnerable.

Again, it's not always obvious.

THE TALK

Based on popular culture, many believe "the talk" is about sex, and in most communities that's true. But in the Black community, there's another talk, and it's about survival.

The talk we get is about the fact that the world will be more difficult for us as Black children as well as adults, and about how to be cautious and respond in situations involving the police or other authorities, who are often white.

For example, we are taught that if we are stopped by a police officer, not to move suddenly, to announce all of our movements, and to speak in ways to make the officer as comfortable as possible. This is an effort to prevent an officer from shooting and killing us.

TULSA RACE MASSACRE

On May 31 and June 1, 1921, mobs of white Tulsa, Oklahoma, residents attacked Black residents in the Greenwood District of the city. The area was known for being the wealthiest Black community in the United States and was often called Black Wall Street.

The attack was carried out from a private plane and on

the ground. White residents dropped bombs, set businesses on fire, beat Black residents to death, and destroyed nearly thirty-five square blocks. This all happened because a Black shoe shiner, Dick Rowland, was accused of assaulting a white woman. When he was taken to the courthouse, rumors began circulating that he had been lynched instead of given due process.

As news spread, race riots began outside the courthouse.

The incident is depicted in the HBO show *Watchmen*, which I recommend you watch. Learn more here: https://www. history.com/topics/roaring-twenties/tulsa-race-massacre.

WHITE PEOPLE ASSUMING BLACK CHILDREN ARE OLDER THAN THEY ARE

One of the most destructive aspects of racism and white supremacy is how Black and brown children are treated and viewed. Unlike other children, many children from these communities aren't presumed to be innocent, young, or still learning. They are seen as dangerous, threatening, and older than they are.

This has been the case in many high-profile instances of racist violence, such as when the murderers of Tamir Rice and Trayvon Martin described their victims as older-looking or frightening when in fact they were just young boys.

This happens with girls as well; from an early age, Black and brown girls are often hypersexualized and treated as if they are women by people outside of their community.

WHITE PRIVILEGE

White privilege is the unearned, built-in, disproportionate access to resources, power, and justice that white people experience over nonwhite people as a result of **systemic racism**.

White privilege is rooted in colonization, though white supremacy has existed since ... well, since "white" has existed, and anything else became "other." These privileges can be small and large. Look into Jane Elliott and her "Blue Eyes/Brown Eyes" exercise (https://janeelliott.com).

You can also read more on white privilege here: https://www.tolerance.org/magazine/fall-2018/what-is-white-privilege-really.

WHITE SAVIOR

A white savior is a white person who uses their privilege and resources to help nonwhite people, but their true reason for doing so is self-serving. On the surface, it may seem as if these people are trying to do something "good," but in reality they are doing it because it helps them in some way.

For example, many white people travel to countries primarily populated by Black and brown people and, while there, take photos of themselves giving money or food to the people who live there. Not only does this perpetuate false narratives about all Black and brown people living in poverty, it's also extremely disrespectful.

White savior moments also fail to account for the fact that opportunities for white people to "help" typically only exist because systems and acts of white supremacy created these conditions of inequality.

WHITE STANDARDS

"White standards" refers to the idea that beauty and cultural norms typically associated with white people are what all racial and cultural groups should aspire to. This notion influences and creates pressure among nonwhite people to alter their appearance, their demeanor, and their own personal culture to fit the ideals that have been aligned with positivity and success in the media and popular culture.

An example of this can be found in the idea of "code-switching," which happens when people adjust the way they speak, look, and/or act in certain settings to fit the standards created by white people and to make white people more comfortable. In many environments, such as the workplace, if nonwhite people fail to code-switch, they are treated as unfit or stereotyped.

WHITE WOMEN'S TEARS

In order to understand the power of white women's tears—which doesn't mean just their tears but also their emotions, reactions, and words—it's important to understand the power that white women wield in our society, whether they're conscious of it or not. This quote by educator Mamta Motwani Accapadi speaks to that point:

> While White women are members of an oppressed group based on gender, they still experience privilege based on race. This dual oppressor/oppressed identity often becomes a root of tension when White women are challenged to consider their White privilege by Women of Color.

The power of white women's tears can be seen in the heinous murder of Emmett Till. In 1955, a white woman named Carolyn Bryant Donham told a group of white men that fourteen-year-old Emmett Till had offended and frightened her by whistling at her.

The men found Emmett and viciously murdered him, then dumped his body in a river. The woman admitted to having lied about it decades later.

Unfortunately, history is full of instances of white women's tears causing outrage and leading to acts of racist violence (like, for example, the **Tulsa Race Massacre**).

WOKENESS

This word is actually in the dictionary! *Merriam-Webster* defines *woke* as being "aware of and actively attentive to important facts and issues (especially issues of racial and social justice)."

XENOPHOBIA

Xenophobia is a hatred or fear of things that are seen as foreign or strange. This is typically manifested as fear of other cultures or ethnic groups based on the presumed purity and/or superiority of one's own group. It is usually related to a fear of the loss of national, ethnic, or racial identity.

PEOPLE AND THINGS TO KNOW

These are people and things I think you should know about. My hope is that you will take the time to google these people, watch some of the TV shows, movies, and documentaries, and read some of the books listed. But don't stop there. Go learn about the people and things referred to here, as well as other people and things similar to these suggestions.

PEOPLE TO LEARN MORE ABOUT

Muhammad Ali

Maya Angelou

James Baldwin

Harry Belafonte

Stokely Carmichael (later known as Kwame Ture)

Shirley Chisholm

Ta-Nehisi Coates

Angela Davis

Ossie Davis

Ruby Dee

Frederick Douglass

Ava DuVernay

Jane Elliott

Marcus Garvey

Langston Hughes

George M. Johnson

Marsha P. Johnson

Spike Lee

Malcolm X (Muslim name el-Hajj Malik el-Shabazz)

Thurgood Marshall

Bree Newsome

THINGS TO READ

Anything by James Baldwin

Anything by Octavia Butler

Anything by Zora Neale Hurston

Anything by Toni Morrison

The Autobiography of Malcolm X by Malcolm X

Between the World and Me by Ta-Nehisi Coates

I Know Why the Caged Bird Sings and other books by
    Maya Angelou

The Souls of Black Folk by W. E. B. Du Bois

Stamped: Racism, Antiracism, and You by Jason Reynolds,
    adapted from *Stamped from the Beginning* by Ibram X.
    Kendi

This Book Is Anti-Racist by Tiffany Jewel, illustrated by
    Aurélia Durand

FREDERICK JOSEPH

THINGS TO WATCH

The Black Panthers: Vanguard of the Revolution
The Color Purple
Do the Right Thing
The Fresh Prince of Bel-Air
Girlfriends
Living Single
Malcolm X
Moonlight
A Raisin in the Sun
13th
Watchmen (**TV series**)
When They See Us

THE BLACK FRIEND PLAYLIST

I couldn't talk about all of that music and not give you something to listen to!

"Grandma's Hands"—Bill Withers

"The Point of It All"—Anthony Hamilton

"The World Is Yours"—Nas **E**

"Tired of Being Alone"—Al Green

"Let's Stay Together"—Al Green

"Naima"—John Coltrane

"Central Park West"—John Coltrane

"Alright"—Kendrick Lamar **E**

"XXX"—FEAT. U2. Kendrick Lamar **E**

"F.U.B.U."—Solange **E**

"Don't Touch My Hair"—Solange **E**

"Borderline (An Ode to Self Care)"—Solange **E**

"Complexion (A Zulu Love)"—Kendrick Lamar **E**

"Formation"—Beyoncé **E**

"Love Bomb" (Album Version, Edited)—N.E.R.D

"Hol' Up"—Kendrick Lamar　🅴

"What's Happening Brother"—Marvin Gaye

"Thinkin Bout You"—Frank Ocean　🅴

"Sweet Life"—Frank Ocean　🅴

"Nikes"—Frank Ocean　🅴

"Self Control"—Frank Ocean

"To Be Young, Gifted and Black"—Donny Hathaway

"Ms. Jackson"—OutKast　🅴

"He Say She Say"—Lupe Fiasco　🅴

"U, Black Maybe"— Common　🅴

"Before I Let Go" (Edit/Remastered)—Maze

"Joy and Pain" (Remastered)—Maze

"Sweet Love"—Anita Baker

"One Step Ahead"—Aretha Franklin

"I Say a Little Prayer"—Aretha Franklin

"Blue in Green"—Miles Davis

"When I Fall in Love"—Miles Davis Quintet

"How's It Goin' Down"—DMX　🅴

"I Do (Cherish You)"—98 Degrees

"Come Close"—Common　🅴

"You Got Me"—The Roots　🅴

"Shook Ones, Pt. II"—Mobb Deep

"The Next Movement"—The Roots　🅴

"Electric Relaxation"—A Tribe Called Quest

"Find a Way"—A Tribe Called Quest

"Renee"—Lost Boyz E

"Sideline Story"—J. Cole E

"4:44"—JAY-Z E

"Legacy"—JAY-Z E

"Umi Says"—Mos Def E

SOURCE NOTES

1: WE WANT YOU TO SEE RACE

pp. 33–34: Scarsdale was listed as the second-wealthiest town in America in 2019: Shelly Hagan and Wei Lu, "These Are the Wealthiest Towns in the U.S.," Bloomberg, February 13, 2019, https://www.bloomberg.com/news/articles/2019-02-13/silicon-valley-suburb-snags-richest-spot-in-u-s-for-third-year.

2: WE CAN ENJOY ED SHEERAN, BTS, AND CARDI B

p. 55: Netflix spent $100 million to keep *Friends*: Edmund Lee, "Netflix Will Keep 'Friends' Through Next Year in a $100 Million Agreement," *New York Times*, December 4, 2018, https://www.nytimes.com/2018/12/04/business/media/netflix-friends.html.

p. 58: Their last album went diamond ... have ever gone diamond: "Top Tallies: Diamond Awards," Recording Industry Association of America (RIAA), https://www.riaa.com/gold-platinum/?tab_active=top_tallies&ttt=DA&col=format&ord=asc#search_section.

p. 69–70: It's also tech... It's statistically proven: See, for instance, Forbes Technology Council, "12 Ways Diversity Makes a Difference in Tech," *Forbes*, July 12, 2018, https://www.forbes.com/sites/forbestechcouncil/2018/07/12/12-ways-diversity-makes-a-difference-in-tech/#7b57541f2bc6.

3: CERTAIN THINGS ARE RACIST, EVEN IF YOU DON'T KNOW IT

p. 88: the persuasive power of personal interactions versus data: See, for instance, Johanne Boisjoly et al., "Empathy or Antipathy? The Impact of Diversity," *American Economic Review* 96, no. 5 (December 2006), https://www.aeaweb.org/articles?id=10.1257/aer.96.5.1890.

4: YOU COULD AT LEAST TRY TO PRONOUNCE MY NAME CORRECTLY

pp. 102–103: proposed bills to limit Chicano, African-American, or Asian-American studies: See, for instance, Kelly McEvers, "Arizona's Ethnic Studies Ban in Public Schools Goes to Trial," *All Things Considered*, NPR, July 14, 2017, https://www.npr.org/2017/07/14/537291234/arizonas-ethnic-studies-ban-in-public-schools-goes-to-trial.

8: NO, I DIDN'T GET HERE BY AFFIRMATIVE ACTION (AND IF I DID, SO WHAT?)

p. 172: affirmative action programs benefiting white women and poor whites more than other groups: See Kimberlé W. Crenshaw, "Framing Affirmative Action," *Michigan Law Review* 105, no. 123 (2206), http://repository.law.umich.edu/mlr_/vol105/iss1/4, and Victoria M. Massie, "White Women Benefit the Most from Affirmative Action—and Are Among Its Fiercest Opponents," Vox, June 23, 2016, https://www.vox.com/2016/5/25/11682950/fisher-supreme-court-white-women-affirmative-action.

p. 173: minority jobholders being more qualified than their supervisors: To read some more about job inequity, see Michael

Gee, "Why Aren't Black Employees Getting More White-Collar Jobs?," *Harvard Business Review*, February 28, 2018, https://hbr.org/2018/02/why-arent-black-employees-getting-more-white-collar-jobs, and Ruqaiijah Yearby, "The Impact of Structural Racism in Employment and Wages on Minority Women's Health," *Human Rights Magazine* 43, no. 3, https://www.americanbar.org/groups/crsj/publications/human_rights_magazine_home/the-state-of-healthcare-in-the-united-states/minority-womens-health/.

9: LET'S NOT DO OPPRESSION OLYMPICS

p. 187: intersections of race, gender, and sexual orientation: For more on this topic, see Jane Coaston, "The Intersectionality Wars," Vox, May 28, 2019, https://www.vox.com/the-highlight/2019/5/20/18542843/intersectionality-conservatism-law-race-gender-discrimination.

10: WE DON'T CARE WHAT YOUR BLACK, BROWN, OR ASIAN FRIEND SAID WAS OKAY (F.U.B.U.)

p. 202: yoga being Hindu-based: "The Yoga Sutras of Patanjali," Internet Encyclopedia of Philosophy, https://www.iep.utm.edu/yoga/.

AN ENCYCLOPEDIA OF RACISM

p. 252: "While White women … Women of Color": Mamta Motwani Accapadi, "When White Women Cry: How White Women's Tears Oppress Women of Color," *College Student Affairs Journal* 26, no. 2 (Spring 2007) 208–215.

ACKNOWLEDGMENTS

First, I want to thank everyone who agreed to take part in this book. You are all some of the most brilliant and passionate people I know. I'm thankful that you were willing to lend your voice and your time.

To my mother, who taught me the joy of reading and equipped me with an ambitious soul. I love you dearly. I am only possible because of you.

To my late grandmother, to whom I promised I would use my talents for good. I hope that I'm making you proud.

My love, Porsche. Thank you for all that you do. You are my partner and friend; it's through our love that all things are possible.

Dre, thank you for all you've done and for being the epitome of working hard for those around you.

My family, which includes far too many to name. Thank you for continuing to believe in me.

Kaylan Adair, my editor and "white friend," ha. You are truly a diamond in the rough. The highest praise I can offer you following the moments I've relived in this book is trust. I trust your talent, your vision, and most of all your heart.

Alex Slater, my literary agent. Thank you for knowing we can shake up the world for years to come and being a thoughtful partner in building lanes for marginalized creators, not just asking for seats.

INDEX

Frederick Joseph is a writer and an award-winning activist, philanthropist, and marketing professional. He was named on the 2019 Forbes 30 Under 30 list, is a recipient of the Bob Clampett Humanitarian Award and was selected for the 2018 Root 100, an annual list of the most influential African Americans. He created the #BlackPantherChallenge and #CaptainMarvelChallenge, philanthropic enterprises enabling disadvantaged young people to watch these groundbreaking films. He has written articles on race, marketing, and politics for outlets such as the *New York Times*, the *Washington Post*, *Essence*, the *Huffington Post*, and the *Root*. He lives in New York City.